Financial Fables

29 stories to help you make smarter decisions about money

By Edwin Palsma

First Printing, 2019

www.financialfablesbook.com

Table of Contents

"If ten coins are not enough to make a man rich, what if you add one coin? What if you add another? Finally, you will have to say that no one can be rich unless one coin can make him so." – Erasmus

Introduction

There once was a thief in India who was on the run from the palace guards. As he was running down a dark alley, he saw a beggar huddled against one of the walls. Quickly, the thief hid the crown jewel he had stolen in one of the beggar's pockets and then ran off. Later that night, the thief was caught and killed. Suddenly, the beggar was the richest man in India, but he didn't know it. He never took the time to look inside his own pocket to see what was there.

CHAPTER AT A GLANCE: Finances is more than just picking good investments. It is about adopting the thought patterns of the financially successful, understanding the financial basics, and learning strategies for smart money management.

Like the beggar, we all have great potential, but we sometimes miss what's right in front of us. We have the capacity to be happy, make good decisions, and live a better life, but poor habits, lack of motivation, and bad luck sometimes get in the way.

I've been lucky to have some great teachers when it comes to money. In my early years, my parents were good examples. They created opportunities to teach my siblings and me about money through paid chores and charging us to use the family car.

I've also benefited from the lessons I've learned as a poor student budgeting my way through university, a project manager making work sites profitable, a primary breadwinner for a family of five, and recently, in the more challenging role of a single parent with support payments.

In my 20 years as a financial professional, I've worked beside many smart people who've taught me how to invest, research, and learn. They've recommended books, resources, and money experts.

These experiences left me with a keen interest in finances and showed me how money can create a better life. Or — through bad choices or luck — a more stressful life. This book is my small attempt to share what I've learned.

I've divided the book into three sections. The first is about changing some of the default programming in our lives – purposefully thinking about money in a way that's more conducive to life and financial success.

An example of changing how we think about money would be, *The Ultimate Gift*, a movie about a billionaire who realizes he's done a poor job teaching his kids and grandkids about the important things in life. The billionaire's family members feel entitled to the family wealth.

The billionaire sets up his will with a Values Trust where, instead of passing his money along, he has one grandson go through a list of twelve tasks that teach him important lessons, better money habits, and offer a more positive outlook on life.

The second part of this book is about basic financial education. Though our schools teach us academic and social skills, financial education is lacking. What schools teach isn't bad, just inadequate. And to be fair, kids aren't typically motivated to learn about finances until they have to. Parents often have an inadequate understanding of finances and fail to pass on good money habits to their children.

The third section is about proven strategies for financial success. Strategies used by famous investors like Warren Buffett, Peter Lynch, and the fictional Richest Man in Babylon.

The last chapter presents an easy way to implement many of these ideas.

And so, we begin...

The Pre-Work

Once a woodcutter strained to saw down a tree. A young man who was watching asked, "What are you doing?"

"Are you blind?" the woodcutter replied. "I'm cutting down this tree."

The young man was unabashed. "You look exhausted! Take a break. Sharpen your saw. If you sharpen the saw, you would cut down the tree much faster."

The woodcutter explained, "I don't have time to sharpen the saw. Don't you see I'm too busy? I've been sawing for hours and do not have time to take a break."

CHAPTER AT A GLANCE: Finances are about the big picture, and knowing yourself is the first part of any plan. This chapter is about knowing where you are and where you want to go.

It's easy to get lost in the day to day. It's normal for us to deal with the next, most urgent thing. But sometimes, especially when it comes to finances, you need to step back and look at the big picture. Cutting down a tree with a dull saw because you don't have time to sharpen it is like never making a long-term plan because work, family, and life get in the way.

In order to know where you're going, you have to know where you are. Start your financial plan: fill out the table below and answer the questions that follow.

Current Situation	
Assets (real estate, pensions, investments)	Debts (mortgages, lines of credit, running credit card debts)
Annual Incomes (jobs, rental income)	Annual Expenses (monthly and annual expenses)
Insurance (Life, Critical Illness, Disability)	Estate Documents (Wills, Powers of Attorney, Health Care Directives)
Do you spend more than you make?	In the last year, has your net worth increased or decreased (assets gone up and liabilities gone down or vice versa)?

Next, list some of your financial responsibilities. If you were to pass away, do you leave a financial hole somewhere? Here is a partial list to get you started.

Financial Responsibilities	
Making money (Are you the sole or partial breadwinner for your family? If you were to pass away, does that leave anyone in financial difficulty?)	Childcare (Are you a stay-at-home parent? If you were to pass away, would your partner have to hire child care?)
Debts (Are there debts left behind if you pass away?)	Education (Do your children have adequate funding for private or post-secondary education?)
Businesses (Do partners rely on your expertise for the running of your business? Do employees rely on you for their jobs?)	Other
Other	Other

The next step is deciding where you want to end up. What are your dreams? What's your version of your perfect future? Here's a table to help you out:

Where will you be living? What subdivision? What type of house? How much is the	

house worth? What are the annual expenses?	
What will your typical retirement day look like? Will you be working part time? What will your hobbies be and how much do they cost?	
What will your vacations look like? Where will you go, how often, what will they cost?	
What sort of legacy are you planning on leaving? How much to children and to charity? What will your friends and family remember you for? Do you want to set up trusts or foundations?	

Now that you know where you're starting from, what your responsibilities are, and where you want to end up, the next step is to calculate the cost of your goals and how much money you'll need to retire. There are many things to consider: inflation, taxes, government benefits, life expectancy, long-term care, legacy, inheritance, savings, etc.

A simple, do-it-yourself way to start is to do an online search for a "retirement planning tool" and choose one of the many financial calculators available. Some of the easiest ones to use are offered by big banks, but simple can also mean limited. If your situation is complicated by inheritances, different retirement ages, part-time work in retirement, legacies, private businesses, real estate holdings, etc., then you may want to engage the services of a financial planner.

If you're currently working with a financial planner, you can sometimes request a personalized plan as part of the services you already pay for. If you're looking for another perspective on your financial plan, it can cost anywhere from $100 to $1,500. Complicated plans that include businesses and trusts can cost upwards of $4,500. In every case, it is worth it.

Planning is starting with where you are and knowing where you need to go. The hardest part of financial planning is the uncertainty and the unknown, which makes it easy to procrastinate.

There are no perfect answers and you'll likely make mistakes. But the biggest mistake is making no financial decisions at all.

WHAT WE LEARNED:

1. Build an accurate picture of your present financial position.
2. Decide where you want to go.
3. Create a financial plan.

Part One:

Perspectives

Thought patterns of the financially successful.

Balance

A squirrel once served a Lion—I know not where or in what capacity. But this much is certain—the Squirrel found favour in the Lion's eyes, and to satisfy a Lion is certainly no small feat. In return for his service the Squirrel was promised a whole wagonload of nuts.

Promised—yes; but meanwhile time continued to fly by. The Squirrel often suffered hunger while grinning in his master's presence, his eyes full of tears.

When he looked around in the forest, his former comrades showed themselves here and there, high up among the trees. The Squirrel watched them—he could do no more than that. At one time, he would be called away; at another, dragged off in the Lion's service.

At last the Squirrel grew old and became tiresome to the Lion. It was time for him to retire. He was granted his discharge, and they actually gave him the full load of nuts—excellent nuts, such as the world had never seen before; all perfect fruit, one as good as another, a perfect marvel. Unfortunately—the Squirrel had long ago lost all his teeth.

CHAPTER AT A GLANCE: Money isn't the most important thing. It's a tool to help us achieve or realize what's most important to us. So — what's important to you?

Balance is today's buzzword. We know we should balance families, health, sleep, spirituality, recreation, work, and finances. This is obvious – but what does it actually mean to find balance?

One of my favourite quotes is from Brian Dyson, the former president and CEO of Coca Cola, who delivered a commencement speech at Georgia Tech:

"Imagine life as a game in which you are juggling five balls in the air. They are called – Work, Family, Health, Friends, and Spirit.

You will soon understand that Work is a rubber ball. If you drop it, it will bounce back. But the other four Balls – Family, Health, Friends, and Spirit – are made of glass. If you drop one of these, they will be irrevocably scuffed, marked, nicked, damaged, or even shattered. They will never be the same."

Balance doesn't mean a lack of focus. Growing up on a farm meant we had to make hay when the sun shone. Sometimes we're called to lay aside distractions and focus on one part of our lives. Unfortunately, like the squirrel, we may become so focused on work, we lose sight of the rest. Or, we focus on having fun and forget to take care of the future.

When we take on many different responsibilities, each pulls us in different directions. When I think about the Apostle Paul from the Bible, he said it was better for him to remain unmarried. He knew the responsibilities of family would distract him from what he felt was his higher calling of being a traveling preacher. Many of us have added spouses and children to our lives, so it's important to make time to do that part right.

To create the right balance, list your responsibilities and priorities. By listing responsibilities — and reviewing them regularly — we're more apt to make wise decisions. Whenever I do this exercise, I'm reminded to spend more time with my kids and friends, and less time on the computer or watching TV. From this sample list of priorities, circle those that apply to you.

Family	Health	Spirituality
Work	Nutrition	Sleep
Mental Health	Education	Parenting
Marriage	Holidays	Volunteering
Renovations	Neighbours	

The next step is to get rid of life's inefficiencies. This might mean less TV or computer games. It might mean working a regular workweek instead of putting in a lot of overtime. It might mean giving up some volunteer commitments or hiring someone to mow the lawn, cook, or clean your house to create more family time.

Below is a list of potential areas of inefficiency. Anything we do to excess can become an inefficiency. For example, exercise is a healthy activity, but too much can take away from other important ways to spend our time. Maybe we spend too much time in each workout session or we hang out at the gym longer than we need to.

TV	Drinking	Video Games
Exercise	Cooking	Reading
House Work	Helping Friends	

Third, ask for a second opinion from a spouse, parent, sibling, or friend. *I* always think I have a good balance. 😊 I love being busy and involved in many things. But thankfully, I have friends who are quick to remind me not to forget my family. There are many days when I should just hang out with family because that time is valuable for both my partner and kids, even if we seem to be getting nothing done.

Fourth, balance includes our finances. While we never know if tomorrow will come, for the vast majority of us, it will (85% of us will live to be 65 and 56% will live to be 80). So it's our responsibility to save for it. In my experience, too many Canadians lean towards spending today. Thankfully, Canada has a safety net for retired people who haven't saved enough themselves. However, the majority of retirees are experiencing a significant drop in their standard of living when they stop working. They have expectations to maintain their lifestyle, and many are struggling.

List three important financial questions or goals you have. Money isn't the most important thing, but it does matter.

#1	
#2	
#3	

Think about your typical week and estimate what percentage of your time (or effort) is being spent in each area of your life. Ranking them is ineffective because today you're in a different season of life than you will be next year. For now, be aware of where you focus your time and decide if it should be more in some areas and less in others.

As the main breadwinner of my family, it's easy to think about finances all the time. But I don't want to have one of those financially successful families that is dysfunctional because Dad was working and never around to play with his kids.

WHAT WE LEARNED:

1. See the big picture.
2. Reflect on what matters most to you.

Values

An old man sold all his goods for a large lump of gold, which he then proceeded to bury in a hole just outside his property. Every day he visited the spot, uncovering the gold, looking at it for a bit, and then covering it back up.

One of the man's employees noticed this odd behavior and followed the old man. He saw the buried gold, and when the old man returned home, the employee removed the gold and ran away with it.

The next day the old man found that his gold was missing and cried out in agony. A neighbor heard the old man's story and suggested that he place a rock in the hole and cover it back up. "It makes no difference, does it? You didn't do anything with the gold anyway."

CHAPTER AT A GLANCE: Money is a tool, not an end goal. Understanding what matters to you lets you use it to have the greatest positive impact in your life.

Having money is great, working hard is important, and saving is essential to having financial success. But like the miser in the fable, if you stop at the money, then what have you gained?

In the *Christmas Carol*, Charles Dickens teaches us about a miser, Scrooge, who lost his humanity because he was so focused on the money. And as a kid, I remember watching cartoons about Scrooge McDuck. I can still see him diving into the money in his vault and swimming among the bills and coins just for the fun of it.

While most of us aren't caught up in the Scrooge mindset, some are. These misers make decisions that have less to do with human experience or deeper values and more to do with accumulating money or stuff.

But on the other extreme, many people don't know what their values are. They spend money on things that don't fully resonate with them. These people go through the motions of life, copying friends and family whether it's tagging along on vacations, buying boats or bigger homes. They haven't spent the time to discover and articulate their own core values.

Back in 2000, when I first started in the financial planning business, I learned a powerful question from an advisor named Bill Bacharach. It starts with "What's important about money to you?" It can be an awkward question — there have been many times that I've sat in silence, waiting to hear the answer. Eventually I hear answers like, "So I can buy stuff," "So I can retire," or "So I can support my family."

The hard part comes next as I replace the word 'money' with their answer. In the first example, that means asking, "What's important about buying stuff, to you?" And so on and so on. There is no right or wrong answer in this set of questions, because it's deeply personal.

And I keep asking the question until the person sitting across from me can't come up with another answer. There will usually be a few more silences as they think about money in a way they never have.

But when we get to that final answer that resonates with them, their ability to make better and more impactful decisions about their finances is realized. The final answer is usually something emotional, not practical which means we've gotten to the depth needed.

I can tell you that I've never taken someone through this and had it stop at the money. Some people haven't wanted to keep going very deep and that's understandable. This is less a logical question and more of an emotional one, so it's normal for it to be uncomfortable.

Part of the challenge of this question is that our perspective on money is framed by our experiences. Going this deep can unlock some negative emotions around what you were taught about money when you were young, either directly or indirectly.

Changing those values is something we will talk about in the next chapter on the Financial Thermostat. But first, you should spend some time thinking about where you are right now. As the question "What's important about money to you?" and see where it leads you.

WHAT WE LEARNED:

1. Money is a tool, not the endgame.
2. Discover your own values, don't copy someone else.

Your Financial Thermostat

One day, a Fox spied a beautiful bunch of ripe grapes hanging from a vine trailing along the branches of a tree. The grapes seemed ready to burst with juice, and the Fox's mouth watered as he gazed longingly at them.

The bunch hung from a high branch and the Fox had to jump for it. The first time he jumped he missed it by a long way. So he walked off a short distance and took a running leap at it, only to fall short once more. Again and again he tried, but his efforts were in vain.

So he sat down and looked at the grapes in disgust. "What a fool I am," he said. "Here I am wearing myself out to get a bunch of sour grapes that are not worth grasping for."

CHAPTER AT A GLANCE: What you think about and how you think about it will become your reality.

The way we choose to view things creates our reality. The Fox created his first reality by salivating over the grapes and then when he couldn't get them, created a new reality by believing the grapes were sour and not worth his time. The Fox's situation didn't change — how he thought about it changed. Similarly, many of us have money challenges because we can't see the potential for a greater life or even imagine the steps to become wealthy.

Harv Ecker, in *Secrets of the Millionaire Mind*, introduced me to the idea of a financial thermostat. Like a thermostat, our subconscious is set to achieve a certain amount of wealth. When we have a low opinion of those with wealth (i.e., when we think of others as filthy rich or believe that money is the root of all evil) then no matter how hard we try, we will never be rich. If we have a positive opinion of those with wealth (i.e., when we think of money as a blessing or that it is the result of hard work) then our subconscious won't subvert our own attempts to become financially successful.

Unfortunately, it's not as simple as wishing we were rich. There are many factors that go into financial success, including hard work, diligence, discipline, and luck. But if your financial thermostat is set low through negative thoughts about money, then hard work and discipline won't be enough.

A good place to start is to look at your friends or your community of people. We typically hang out in certain socioeconomic groups because we can afford to do the same things (travel, golf, etc.) as they can. When you look at your circle of friends, whom do you see? Are they trying to look wealthy (the pseudo rich)? Are they hard workers? Do they complain about their finances? Are they opportunistic?

Hanging out with rich people doesn't make you rich, but I can tell you that hanging out with the pseudo rich will keep you poor. Looking rich by buying all the right toys, living in the right neighbourhood, and going on the right vacations are not things you want to emulate.

A friend told me about his visit to a market in Jamaica where a vendor was selling parrots. These parrots were calmly sitting on their perches, but they weren't tied down. When asked why they didn't fly away, the vendor explained that the parrots are taught from a young age that the perch is a place of safety, which makes them afraid to fly away. Similarly, elephants that are chained to a stump as babies will not pull away when chained to a small post as adults, because they've been conditioned to believe that a chain around their ankle is inescapable.

What we learn about finances at a young age can trap us into poor thinking and bad habits. Learning to recognize these beliefs and growing with our changing financial situation is very important.

Financially, a prime example of not adapting are lottery winners. A study by Scott Hankins, et al[1], showed that larger windfalls do not reduce, but only delay the likelihood of bankruptcy. Over my years as a financial planner, two meetings with potential clients stand out. Their net worth compared to the way they talked just didn't seem to fit. Their financial perspective and knowledge didn't align with their wealth. One couple had in fact won the lottery and the other had received a large inheritance. In each case, their concern was that their money was flowing out faster than they thought it should so they were looking for help.

They were hoping for an easy solution or a magic investment that would make them high returns for no risk. They hadn't learned that it takes hard work combined with good decision making to earn wealth and then to subsequently keep and grow it.

Their thermostat was set to low wealth because they hadn't learned the principles you will read about in this book. Maybe they had poor modeling from parents or they refused to put in the effort. As a result, they were overspending and making poor financial decisions. I presented them with some practical solutions, the most important of which was to spend only what they made. But they were looking for an easier path and, consequentially, I never saw them again.

On the other hand, we've all known people who make it rich, go bankrupt, and then make it rich again. What makes them different? The next few chapters will talk about mindsets and thought patterns to set your financial thermostat higher.

Henry Ford said, "Whether you think you can or you can't, you are right." Our mind is our most powerful tool and having it focused on the right things makes all the difference.

WHAT WE LEARNED:

1. Have the right attitude.
2. Examine who you hang out with.
3. Learn a better way to think about money.

Opportunity Mentality

When the great library of Alexandria burned, the story tells that one book was saved. But it was not a valuable book; and so a man, who could read a little, bought it for a few pennies. The book wasn't very interesting, but between its pages there was something very valuable indeed. It was a thin strip of vellum on which was written the secret of the 'Touchstone!'

The Touchstone was a small pebble that could turn any common metal into pure gold. The book explained that it was lying among thousands and thousands of other pebbles on the shore that looked exactly like it. But the secret was this; the real stone would feel warm, while ordinary pebbles are cold. So the man sold his few belongings, bought some simple supplies, camped on the seashore, and began testing pebbles.

He knew that if he picked up ordinary pebbles and threw them down again because they were cold, he might pick up the same pebble hundreds of times. So, when he felt one that was cold, he threw it into the sea. He spent a whole day doing this but none of them was the Touchstone.

Yet he went on and on this way. Pick up a pebble. Cold – throw it into the sea. Pick up another. Throw it into the sea.

The days stretched into weeks and the weeks into months. One day, however, about mid-afternoon, he picked up a pebble and it was warm. He threw it into the sea before he realized what he had done. He had formed such a strong habit of throwing each pebble into the sea that when the one he wanted came along, he still threw it away.

CHAPTER AT A GLANCE: Pause and be mindful of what's going on around you. Getting lost in the day to day is just that – getting lost.

What makes many wealthy people different from the average person (more than just their wealth) is that they think differently. They look at life as a series of opportunities, instead of a series of impossible challenges. They wake up thinking about the opportunities that will come their way. This is not to say wealthy people are always successful, but because they think differently, their subconscious is working with them. Instead of going through the motions of daily life, people with an opportunity mentality walk with their heads up and eyes open.

The man in the story above got so used to the motion of picking up stones and throwing them in the ocean that he stopped paying attention to what he was doing. We've all experienced life on autopilot, whether it's waking up one day and wondering how our kids got so old or driving to work and not remembering a single thing from the trip.

A friend of mine recently lost his job. He told me he was choosing to see this as the start of a new opportunity. As a professional counselor, he'd always encouraged his patients to see life as a series of opportunities. So when he found himself in a jam, he chose this same belief.

As we talked, it was amazing how in just a week, at a time when unemployment was higher than average, he had a half dozen good ideas for jobs and the connections to pursue them. He connected with many friends who had ideas for new opportunities. Before he lost his job, he was always upgrading his skills which meant he wasn't limited to looking for the same job again.

Some of the most successful investors I've met are the same as this friend of mine. They see a fall in stock or real-estate prices differently as an opportunity to buy up a good investment at a good price. I know an investor who loves to own gold and he's excited when gold prices fall because he buys more every month. Another friend saw huge opportunity and invested heavily in Calgary real estate in the early 1990s when people were selling low to escape the city.

Opportunity people take risks. Michael Jordan was one of the most clutch basketball players of all time. He wanted the ball in the dying seconds of a game with the potential winning shot in *his* hands. He knew he'd miss many shots, but not taking the shot guaranteed 100% failure. So where other players would have rather passed the ball, Michael Jordan took the shot.

Opportunity people don't want to miss anything — they walk with their heads up and engage the world.

Here are some ways to become opportunity focused:

- At school: What can I do to challenge myself? If I think about successful people I'd like to emulate, which courses could I be taking to be like them? Which courses will help me the most in my chosen field of study?

- At work: Are there other jobs in my field that have more opportunity? What skills could I learn to move up the hierarchy? How can I become more valuable to my employer?
- At investing: Of the successful people I know, who can I talk to? Can my financial advisor point me to places where I can learn more? Are there local courses taught by successful investors?
- When networking: How can I meet more people and engage with them more effectively?

So how do you look at the world? What's next? What's around the corner? What could be amazing?

WHAT WE LEARNED:

1. Be aware if you are stuck in a rut.
2. Look for opportunities everywhere.
3. Have a desire to learn and be challenged.

Positivity #1: Optimism

One very stormy day a Poor Man came to a Rich Man's house to beg.

"Away with you!" said the servants. "Do not come here troubling us."

In response, the Poor Man said, "Only let me come in and dry my clothes at your fire." This, the servants thought, would not cost them anything, so they let him come in.

The Poor Man then asked the cook to let him have a pan, so that he could make some stone broth.

"Stone broth!" said the cook. "I should like to see how you can make broth out of a stone." So she handed him a pan. The Man filled it with water from the pump, and then put into it a stone from the road. "But you must have some salt," said the cook.

"Do you think so?" courteously replied the stranger. The cook gave him the salt, and before long she added some peas, some mint, and thyme. At last she brought him all the scraps of meat she could find, so that the Poor Man's broth made him a good dinner.

"You see," said the Poor Man, "that if you try long enough, are cheerful, and make the best of what you have, you may at last get what you want."

CHAPTER AT A GLANCE: Optimism is the first of three aspects of positivity. Realistic optimists do better in life. They're smarter, more perceptive, and more likable, all of which are keys to financial success.

Optimism is the first of three mindsets in the category of positivity, the others being gratitude and generosity. The definition of positivity is not the same as happiness (though there's a strong link). Positivity isn't about grinning and bearing it or just looking on the bright side of life. I define positivity as seeing life as *happy, punctuated by temporary, difficult events* as opposed to seeing life as *difficult, punctuated by temporary happy events.*

Optimistic people approach life expecting good things to happen. This mindset is epitomized by the Poor Man in the fable above. He approached a cold, hungry night believing it could only get better. He acted as if the evening would work out and it did.

You can see a full summary of the benefits of optimism studies at https://www.verywellmind.com/the-benefits-of-optimism-3144811.

Being optimistic increases our cognitive abilities. We're literally smarter when we are in a happier state. Optimism makes us look younger. Optimism attracts others to us. Optimistic leaders get more out of their teams. Optimistic students get better grades. Optimistic people are more financially successful.

Optimistic people also live longer. In 1991, researchers at the University of Pittsburgh analyzed 97,253 women who'd never had cancer or cardiovascular disease. When they did a follow up study eight years later, those women identified as being in the most optimistic fifth were 28% less likely to contract a cardiovascular disease and had 27% less chance of dying from all causes than the most pessimistic fifth.

Hillary Tindale, author of that study, stated that optimistic people are more likely to seek medical advice and follow it. Studies show optimists are inclined to stick with diet programs prescribed by their doctors and "have good social networks and strong social relationships." All of which helps them cope with chronic stress, a risk factor for heart disease.

Stress is the leading cause of illness among Canadians, and optimists are usually able to handle stress better. Whether this is because they have a larger social network to lean on or because their optimism creates a mind over matter phenomenon is unknown. In her TED talk, Kelly McGonigal points out that it's not the absence of stress that categorizes healthier people, but their perspective of stress. People who viewed stress as a part of life and something that could make them stronger ended up as healthier individuals.

In another study on optimism from 2005-2007, researchers from the Fuqua School of Business and Yale School of Management compared the job-hunting success of recent MBA graduates. They found that the more optimistic students found jobs quicker and easier. In a follow-up study two years later, those same optimists were more likely to be promoted than their more pessimistic colleagues.

The study highlighted that optimists tend to appear more charismatic and social, which partially contributed to their success. The researchers posited that people who are optimistic by disposition are better at coping with problems and more flexible about trying new courses of action when needed.

A report by Julia K. Boehm and Sonja Lyubomirsky in 2008 found a correlation between happiness and workplace success. They asked which comes first: the success or the happiness (like the age old chicken or the egg question). Common belief is that one must first attain some sort of success and then happiness will follow. However, the finding of the study revealed the exact opposite. Those who were the happiest achieved the greater measure of success.

This goes back to the argument of nature vs. nurture; are we a product of our genes or our environment? Some studies have shown that happiness is somewhat genetic and that we have pre-set levels of happiness built into our brains. But within that, we appear to have wiggle room and one's "happiness bar" can grow or shrink. So what can you do to raise your happiness?

In *The Happiness Advantage*, author Shawn Achor states that, "Happiness is not a mood. It's a work ethic." This statement has dramatically changed how I go about my daily life — I don't wait around for circumstances or someone to make me feel happy. The work is in choosing to be happy first and then living my life second. Because numerous studies show that our brain works better when it's in a better state of mind, here are ten strategies to become more positive:

1. **Meditate for five minutes a day.** Pay attention to your breathing – watch it go in and out. When your mind wanders, which it will do, gently bring it back to think about your breathing. I've been working on this off and on for six years and I find that after those five minutes, I feel more relaxed, refreshed, and at ease.
2. **Invest in relationships.** A person's loneliness is correlated to their happiness. Studies show that people with a larger or deeper social circle are happier.
3. **Smile more.** An interesting study showed that when holding a pencil in their teeth (forcing the smiling muscles to activate), people found cartoons funnier than when they held the pencil under their nose like a mustache (forcing frowning muscles to activate).
4. **Manage Stress.** This suggestion isn't about eliminating stress, because that is impossible. If you view life as joyful with small periods of stress as opposed to life being stressful with small periods of joy, this will contribute to your happiness.
5. **Find something to look forward to every day.** Whether it's an upcoming vacation, coffee with a close friend, seeing your kids at the end of a work day, or getting to the gym, anticipation of a positive future event causes your brain to release serotonin into your bloodstream and makes you feel better.
6. **Commit to conscious acts of kindness.** This isn't about reflecting at the end of the day and thinking about five things you've done. It has to be premeditated and deliberate. Have a kind word for a co-worker. Pay for a coffee for the next person in line at Tim Hortons. Email

someone with a word of thanks for something they did long ago.

7. **Infuse your surroundings with positivity.** At your desk, have pictures of family or places you really like. Go for regular walks, even if it's just around the block, and pay attention to the nature around you. Watch less TV. Those who watch the news have a more negative and inaccurate view of the world.
8. **Exercise.** It helps you control your weight. It builds the ability to focus. It also causes your brain to release serotonin into your bloodstream. It gives you self-confidence as you develop skills in a particular area.
9. **Spend money on others and/or experiences, not on stuff.** Studies show that when people are given free money and then told to do one of three things – spend money on themselves, spend money on others, or spend money on experiences — the latter two groups had higher levels of happiness and satisfaction than the former. Spending money on others and on experiences makes a huge difference to one's well-being.
10. **Focus on a signature strength**. There is a great sense of satisfaction that comes from doing something you are good at. It's good for your brain to experience successes on a regular basis because so much of our lives are filled with hard work where the benefits may not be obvious (such as raising kids). Go to www.viasurvey.org for a survey that will help you identify some of your core strengths.

When we choose to approach life with optimism, we often find ourselves happier. And if we are happier, we will be more motivated and in a better state of mind to make good financial decisions.

WHAT WE LEARNED

1. Approach life with as much optimism as possible to improve what actually happens in your life.
2. Actively use strategies that will result in more optimism.

Positivity #2: Gratitude and Thankfulness

A slave named Androcles once escaped from his master and fled to the forest. As he was wandering about he came upon a Lion lying on the ground, moaning and groaning. At first he turned to flee, but finding that the Lion did not pursue him, he turned back and went up to him. As he came near, the Lion put out his paw, which was swollen and bleeding. Androcles found that a huge thorn had gotten into it and was causing all the pain.

He pulled out the thorn and bound up the paw of the Lion, who was soon able to rise and lick the hand of Androcles like a dog. Then the Lion took Androcles to his cave, and every day he brought him meat to eat. But shortly afterwards, both Androcles and the Lion were captured, and the slave was sentenced to be fed to the Lion after the latter had been kept without food for several days.

The Emperor and his Court came to see the spectacle, and Androcles was led out into the middle of the arena. Soon the Lion was let loose from his den and rushed bounding and roaring towards his victim. But as soon as he came near to Androcles he recognized his friend, and fawned upon him, licking Androcles's hands like a friendly dog.

The Emperor, surprised at this, summoned Androcles, who

told him the whole story, whereupon the slave was pardoned and freed, and the Lion let loose to his native forest.

CHAPTER AT A GLANCE: Gratitude shifts your perspective from one of scarcity and poverty to one of abundance and riches. You start to see more options and other ways of doing things.

Gratitude, or thankfulness, is the second characteristic of positivity. It is about having an appreciation for life! Gratitude is about the big picture, about seeing the good in life instead of focusing on the negative.

Gratitude has a ripple effect. The slave in the story above, thankful for not being eaten by the lion, investigated why. The lion, thankful that his paw had been fixed, fed the slave. And together, these actions resulted in freedom for both of them.

In most cases, gratitude is expressed or felt for something someone does for us. I would suggest that it should go beyond that and be expressed or felt about our own circumstances in life. In *The Rational Optimist*, Matt Ridley compares our living standards to people who lived hundreds of years ago. The average Canadian today has a higher standard of living than the richest person even just 200 years ago. Yet, due to the powerful effects of media and advertising, we are more likely to feel we are lacking something, rather than feel contentment with and even awe for the amazing world in which we live.

In her book *Inspire Your Career*, Patricia Barbato impressed me with how she wrote about gratitude so I'm including an excerpt:

"Cultivating gratitude shifts your perspective from one of scarcity and poverty to one of abundance and riches. You start to see more options and more ways of doing things. Instead of having feelings of frustration and anger for what you have lost or do not have, you shift to feelings of appreciation for what you have gained and what you do have. One day you find yourself stewing over the fact that your colleague's work was recognized at the team meeting. You feel you did just as much as she did and can't understand why you didn't get the same acknowledgment. The bitterness starts to build a wall of resentment and anger that isolates you from your colleagues and boss. You build up a sense of scarcity and poverty, as if there is not enough appreciation to share. It is as if the recognition your colleague received takes away from the recognition that is available to you. In such situations, draw on your gratitude. In the same example, you can feel appreciative of what your colleague accomplished, congratulate her, and be thankful for the opportunity to see how someone else excelled and was recognized for their achievements. This approach builds the feeling of abundance and richness and gives the impression that there is enough recognition for everyone and that everyone can excel. The next time a situation occurs, even if it is negative, ask, "What can I be grateful for in this situation?"

As Patricia writes, gratitude is about perspective. On a daily basis, it's about choosing to look at situations in a positive light. Not only does this help improve our mood, but it draws other people to us, which can also be a source of happiness.

In her next section, Patricia goes on to discuss the importance of seeing the bigger picture. If you are reading this book, you are likely living in Canada which means you won the global lottery. We have access to clean water, good food, universal healthcare, and safety. The day to day can seem so difficult, but stepping back and seeing the forest instead of the trees makes a huge difference.

One of the reasons I respect Warren Buffett, other than his obvious investment acumen, is his willingness to acknowledge that a key part of his success was being born at a time of opportunity in a country that afforded him the luxury of being an investment manager. He has this attitude despite (or maybe because of) being born during the Great Depression. And this gratitude has inspired him to give away the majority of his wealth when he dies. It also inspired him to approach other wealthy people like Bill Gates to encourage them to become philanthropists too.

Living with gratitude has huge benefits. It draws people to us as they see in our attitude something they want to have themselves. Gratitude makes the world a better place because grateful people are nicer, more caring, and make a difference in our world.

As in the fable above, the benefits of gratitude aren't always clear. The attitude of gratitude of both the lion and Androcles created a partnership that ultimately led to both being freed. For you, it may take years for that chance meeting or that favour you did to result in something good for you. Because life is better when you live in a state of gratitude and thankfulness.

WHAT WE LEARNED:

1. Appreciate the life you have.
2. Embrace abundance and not a scarcity or poverty attitude.
3. See the big picture.

Positivity #3: Generosity

Once when a Lion was asleep a little Mouse began running up and down upon him; this soon woke up the Lion, who placed his huge paw upon the Mouse, and opened his big jaws to swallow him.

"Pardon me, O King," cried the little Mouse, "please forgive me this time and I shall never forget it. Who knows? I may be able to do you a good turn one day."

The Lion was so tickled at the idea of the Mouse being able to help him that he lifted up his paw and let him go.

Sometime later the Lion was caught in a trap. The hunters who desired to carry him alive to the King tied him to a tree while they went in search of a wagon. Just then the little Mouse happened to pass by, and seeing the sad plight of the Lion, went up to him and gnawed away the ropes that bound the King of the Beasts.

"Was I not right?" asked the little Mouse.

CHAPTER AT A GLANCE: Generosity is doing good deeds. It has mental benefits, it draws people to you, and creates useful connections and friendships.

This third characteristic of positivity, generosity, is what I call gratitude in action. Generosity flows naturally from someone who is filled with gratitude and realizes the benefits they have already received. It is giving something of yourself (time, money or advice) that in general results in little or no benefit to you.

Similar to the previous chapter, the act of generosity has many benefits that are not always readily apparent. Many times, it's a matter of faith that our actions will be reciprocated in the future, like the Mouse in the fable. I'm not saying give to get, but the energy that surrounds a generous person is noticeable.

Movies like *Pay it Forward* and *The Ultimate Gift* give concrete examples of how generosity benefits society; it creates feelings of community, starts chain reactions, and changes people.

Our health is positively impacted as well. A recent study by Dr. Marco Iacoboni, a professor of psychiatry at the David Geffen School of Medicine at UCLA, found that our brains are hard wired more for generosity than selfishness. When we give, our bodies produce serotonin which is a key chemical for health. Serotonin aids our ability to learn and memorize; it facilitates digestion, it regulates our sleep, and it's a main driver of our moods. So, cheerful giving begets cheerfulness.

I'm not a great believer in mysticism, but the concept of Karma makes sense to me. People who give generally find that they get something back. It isn't as simple as giving $10 to the homeless man on the street and suddenly you find an unexpected $100 cheque in the mail.

Rather, givers attract people and situations that improve their lives. Generosity, gratitude, and optimism are parts of a circle, each building on the other. Givers tend to see the glass as half full – they see opportunities where others see challenges. They take advantage of situations instead of missing them.

Givers attract other givers. I used to sit on the board of Big Brothers Big Sisters of the Fraser Valley. When we were in need of a new building, the initial donors who stepped up were able to connect us to other donors, who connected us with even more donors. Through this process, the donors strengthened existing business relationships and formed new relationships.

Generosity comes back to Warren Buffet's philosophy of having an attitude of gratitude. By being Canadian, the cosmic dice rolled in your favour, and one way to acknowledge our luck is to be charitable.

The least compelling but still valuable benefit is that giving results in favourable tax treatment. Because society recognizes the societal good of charities, governments encourage charitable donations by giving a tax deduction on any donations made to a registered charity, cutting the cost of donating in half. This ensures that there is no tax penalty for giving away money. While giving money away rarely results in an equal monetary benefit, the other benefits still make it worthwhile.

WHAT WE LEARNED:

1. Do good deeds because it will pay off (though not always in obvious ways).
2. Be generous to be healthier and to make good connections with other generous people.

Work and Work Ethic

The Ants and the Grasshoppers lived together in the great field. The Ants were busy all the time gathering a store of grain to lay by for winter use. They gave themselves so little pleasure that their merry neighbours, the Grasshoppers, began at last to take no notice of them.

When the frost came, it put an end to the work of the Ants and the chirping and merrymaking of the Grasshoppers. But one fine winter's day, when the Ants were employed in spreading their grain in the sun to dry, a Grasshopper, who was nearly perishing with hunger, chanced to pass by.

"Good day to you, kind neighbour," said she; "will you not lend me a little food? I will certainly pay you before this time next year."

"How does it happen that you have no food of your own?" asked an old Ant. "There was an abundance in the field where we lived side by side all summer, and your people seemed to be active enough. What were you doing?"

"Oh," said the Grasshopper, forgetting his hunger, "I sang all the day long, and all the night, too."

"Well, then," interrupted the Ant, "I must not deprive my own family for you. If Grasshoppers find it so pleasurable to sing away the summer, they must starve in winter," and she went

on with her work, all the while singing the old song, "We ants never borrow; we ants never lend."

CHAPTER AT A GLANCE: Hard work brings success.

This is one of the most well-known fables in the world. When I looked it up, I had forgotten that the fable has the ant shunning the grasshopper and letting him starve. I guess most parents and teachers leave that part out as it's too shocking for young minds.

But for you, my adult reader, this is a reality. In the vast majority of cases, hard work is well-rewarded and being lazy isn't.

Napoleon Hill, in his famous book *The Laws of Success* specifies one of the laws as "The Habit of Doing More than [You are Being] Paid For." This habit works because you are building up many good things – habits, work ethic, and respect. People see these character traits and are drawn to you. They want to work with you because they see that you get things done.

This habit makes one more valuable as an employee. When there is a promotion to be had, who gets it? When there are cutbacks to be made, who doesn't get fired? And if this makes you think about nepotism, then go back and reread my chapter on the financial thermostat.

Building this habit is a life-long endeavor, not something you should try for a few months. Your bosses, co-workers and colleagues can see right through it if you are trying to game your way through this habit. It has to be something you believe and live every day. This is a habit you can't fake.

In adults who epitomize hard work, I see an attitude of enjoying the journey. Many people are not willing to try something new or they're more worried about appearances than about success or learning. This fear of failure keeps many people from looking at their finances. They procrastinate because they feel helpless and think they won't be rich anyways. This results in hoping and wishing for the winning lottery ticket. Rather, view your finances as a part of your journey where a few small decisions can have a huge impact.

As a parent, I spend a lot of time thinking about raising great kids. It feels like an impossible task because so much is out of my control. But one thing I can control is how I talk to my children. In a 1998 study by Carol Dweck and Claudia Mueller, 5th graders were tested on the effect of praising children for hard work or for success. The results were clear. Children praised for success were less likely to try a new task or attempt the harder test. If you praise success, your children will look for shortcuts or easy jobs. The fear of failure will override the excitement of a challenge.

Instead, children who were praised for their hard work were more likely to attempt the harder test and persevered longer on that test.

So how do you go about your work every day? Regardless of what you do, a paying job, being a parent, or going to school, it should be taken seriously. 'If you are going to do something, you might as well do it well,' is an adage I've heard many times. You will reap the benefits.

WHAT WE LEARNED:

1. Choose hard work and it will soon become a habit.
2. Find ways to enjoy your work to make it easier and more fulfilling.

Constant Learning

A Fox and a Hedgehog were out walking one day. They started to talk about their respective ways of not getting caught by the eagles.

The Fox started to regale the Hedgehog with stories about all the ways he had successfully escaped the clutches of the eagle, from running down into other animals' burrows, to hiding in the long grass, to running up a tree and hiding among the branches.

The Hedgehog said that he knew only one thing, but it was a big thing. He would curl into a ball and let his prickly spines deter any would-be predator. They each debated the merits of their respective strategies but neither managed to convince the other.

CHAPTER AT A GLANCE: The world is getting smarter so we have to keep up. It's what will differentiate us from others – because what we know today will not be enough to win the day tomorrow.

This is one of my favourite fables, because it highlights that there are many ways to solve a problem. While knowing one big thing (like the Hedgehog) can work, life today is too complicated for that mentality. There's always something more to discover and circumstances change. As I continue to learn, I realize there's just so much I don't know. And with some scientists estimating that young people today will be able to live to 120 years old (and quality years at that), I start to get excited about how much more I will get to learn over the next 80 years!

I see many people who say they can't keep up, that it's too hard, and that the world needs to just slow down. Not my mom. I love her ability to constantly push herself. Whether it's learning how to Skype so she can see her grandchildren, joining a dancing club, zip lining over a pool of alligators, or riding an ostrich, she experiences life. She's up for babysitting three kids under the age of seven for nine days, painting two rooms when she's visiting us from Alberta, and taking her motorcycle out for a spin with a bunch of people she doesn't even know. My mom works at learning new things all the time.

Moore's Law states that the pace of change is constantly accelerating. Thousands of years ago, it took many generations for a major change to happen, such as humans evolving from hunters to gatherers to farmers. Decades ago, it took a generation to move from washing clothes by hand to washing machines. And now, it only takes years to move from phone to cell phone to smart phone.

What does this mean for us? Many things we learned in school are obsolete (remember when Pluto was a planet?). And the things our kids are learning in school will be old news after they graduate. Keeping up is not about being smart, but about being open to change. The most successful people in the future will be those ready to accept the new things that crop up.

But the human default is to seek out comfort which is usually the antithesis of change. We surround ourselves with familiarity and routine; the same people, the same books, the same news.

Republicans spend the majority of their TV time listening to Fox News, NDPers listen to CBC, christians listen to Christian talk shows, atheists listen to atheist talk shows, and doomsdayers listen to other extremists. All this does is perpetuate current thinking rather than inform or increase knowledge and wisdom.

This is sometimes perpetuated by something called a filter bubble. As internet programs learn of your search interests and habits, the programs start to deliver more and more information that agrees with you, rather than showing you multiple perspectives on an issue. This soon becomes a self-fulfilling cycle where you feel more and more certain about your opinions.

To be a successful investor requires the ability to accept that things change — an investment that's good today isn't necessarily going to be good tomorrow. While some things never change (investment principles like diversification and discipline), many things do change (tax law, income splitting, interest rates, economic environment, etc.). So keeping up is about being adaptable, paying attention, and not getting stuck in the mud. It's about being a fox and not a hedgehog.

The most successful investors are always reading, listening, and watching. Whether it's Warren Buffett, Peter Lynch, George Soros, or my friends Chris and Nathan, information gathering is a critical component to success. They acknowledge that the world isn't black and white. It's filled with differing opinions and it's always changing, so investors have to keep learning.

Something I've incorporated into my investment research is to listen or read comments each week from at least two people with whom I disagree. When I'm reading, I'm not just trying to poke holes in their thoughts. I try to take time to see things from their points of view. It's hard work to disagree with yourself but it's a good mental exercise. So spend more time listening and learning from diverse ideas as opposed to trying to find information that confirms your already held beliefs.

WHAT WE LEARNED:

1. Embrace change.
2. Have a variety of interests.
3. Acknowledge your own ignorance and try to change it.

Decision Fatigue

"Oh Father," said a Little Frog to the Big one sitting by the side of a pool, "I have seen such a terrible monster! It was as big as a mountain, with horns on its head, a long tail, and it had hooves divided in two."

"Hush, child," said the Father Frog, "that was only Farmer White's Ox. It isn't so big either; he may be a little bit taller than I, but I could easily make myself quite as broad. Just you see." So he blew himself out, and blew himself out, and blew himself out. "Was he as big as that?" asked he.

"Oh, much bigger than that," said the young Frog.

Again the old one blew himself out, and asked the young one if the Ox was as big as that.

"Bigger, Father, bigger," was the reply.

So Father Frog took a deep breath, and blew and blew and blew, and swelled and swelled and swelled. And then he said: "I'm sure the Ox is not as big as…" But at this moment he burst.

CHAPTER AT A GLANCE: The energy to make decisions is a limited resource, so use it wisely. Make tough decisions in the morning. Limit the decisions you need to make each day to save energy for the important decisions and work to strengthen your decision making muscles.

Small stressful things add up, potentially becoming a larger burden. Each little breath Father Frog took, limited his ability to take another, until he burst. Each breath is like a small decision we make, adding up until we can't make one more – or, until we collapse under the stress of all those small decisions.

Studies show we have a limited amount of self-control and the more we use it in a day, the less we have of it later on. If you've ever tried fasting or dieting, you most likely became more irritable and less patient. Decision-making is a part of self-control. When we make many small decisions, we use up our daily decision making capacity. Then, if we have to make a big decision later in the day, our ability to see the big picture or to delay gratification is harder.

Paul Tough, in his book *How Children Succeed* explains why people struggle so much when trying to escape poverty. People living on the edge of poverty are forced to spend their daily mental energy on scraping by, trying to make a living, worrying about budgets, and paying bills. And this often means that at the end of the day, when the kids are finally in bed, they have less time and mental energy to think long-term. Part of the poverty cycle, as he explains, is that because of the daily grind people go through just to survive, they have less time and energy to spend taking their children to extracurricular events, teaching them good work habits, or helping them deal with stress.

People who have to make really big decisions, such as Fortune 500 CEOs and heads of state, know that mental energy is a limited resource, so they hire people to make basic decisions for them. In the case of US Presidents, many of them let others pick out their wardrobe, what they'll eat, when and whom to meet, etc. This ensures that they have adequate energy and clarity to help with the big decisions when they come up.

We're so inundated with daily decisions that when it comes time to make big ones, we just don't have the energy. If you've been lifting boxes all day, your arms will get tired. Your brain is just like every other muscle; you can strengthen it and you can wear it out. So here are some decision-making tips with respect to money:

1. **Make important money decisions early in the day.** Do not make a decision when you are tired, hungry, or distracted. As the day goes on, more things will have come across our plate. Our brains might be filled with thoughts that take away from our focus on the important decision at hand. Being hungry is also bad as studies show that decisions made just before lunch or dinner are more likely to be a default decision, as we are impatient to get it over with, rather than wanting to take the time to make the best decision possible.
2. **Think about the impact of a decision using the 10-10-10 rule.** Think about the impact of a decision over three time frames: 10 minutes, 10 months, and 10 years putting particular emphasis on the 10-year time frame. For example, when buying that must-have pair of jeans, will it make a difference in your life in the next 10

minutes? 10 months? 10 years? Usually, you'll find that a pair of $50 jeans will work just as well as the $200 pair that you really want. By the same token, will increasing your monthly savings by $100 a month have an impact on your finances in 10 minutes? 10 months? 10 years?

3. **Pretend a friend is asking you the question.** What advice would you give them? This helps because sometimes we get lost in our own situation, but if we pull back and treat the decision as if it's someone else's, we can gain clarity and make a more thoughtful, less emotional decision.
4. **Limit the number of places where you save money.** Have one bank and one financial advisor. This makes it easier to keep track of things in your head.
5. **Limit the number of credit cards and loyalty cards you have.** It's mentally taxing to keep track and manage all of them.
6. **Set up rules that will limit your need to make decisions.** Things like automatic bill payments and daily spending limits (i.e., you can't buy anything that costs more than $200 until 3 days have passed).
7. **Set up your savings to be automatic.** To be especially proactive, automatically deposit savings regularly so you don't have to decide on that day.
8. **Be aware of self-herding.** Have you ever been in an unfamiliar neighbourhood and looked for a restaurant? You likely picked the busiest because obviously people like it – this is called herding. Self-herding is when we do what we've done in the past. For example, many of us stop for a coffee before heading into work. The first time we did it, we probably thought about the pros and cons

of that choice. But the next time we are faced with that choice, we didn't do as much thinking. We bought a coffee yesterday and it was a good decision then, so it's probably a good decision today.

9. **Get help.** How much practice do you have in making big decisions like buying houses, cars, or investments? There are professionals who spend every day immersed in these big decisions so they get good at them. They learn to recognize the important part of each decision and are less distracted by the inconsequential parts of the decision-making process. Or, call on a friend or family member who has gone through the same thing before.

WHAT WE LEARNED:

1. Make important decisions early in the day.
2. Limit the number of decisions you make in a day by creating habits for the easy stuff.
3. Be thoughtful about how you spend your money – don't mindlessly copy your previous decisions.

Part Two:

Knowledge

Making sense of financial basics

Right Spending

One day a farmer going to the nest of his Goose found an egg all yellow and glittering. When he took it up it was as heavy as lead. He was going to throw it away because he thought a trick had been played upon him, but he took it home and soon found, to his delight, that it was an egg of pure gold. Every morning the same thing occurred, and he soon became rich by selling his eggs. As he grew rich he grew greedy; and thinking to get at once all the gold the Goose could give, he killed it and opened his belly only to find nothing.

CHAPTER AT A GLANCE: Rich people (and those on their way to getting rich) spend less than they make – all the time!

Focusing on material possessions and overspending are the two most common mistakes of the financially unsuccessful. Like the farmer who wasn't satisfied with what he had, we kill our personal Golden Goose by strangling it with debt. It isn't easy to be patient, but there can be a huge payoff at the end.

One of my favourite financial books of all time is Thomas Stanley's *The Millionaire Next Door*. Among the many truths in the book, the critical one is that appearances are deceiving; just because a person looks wealthy, doesn't mean they actually are.

In doing his research, Dr. Stanley sent special dinner invitations to those people who lived in the wealthiest parts of town and to those with the highest incomes such as doctors, dentists, and lawyers.

What Dr. Stanley found was shocking: most of these people were not millionaires. Rather, their large incomes were used to finance their expensive lifestyle. While they did earn lots of money (in most cases they were in the top 2% of income earners in town), they didn't have much real wealth to show for it.

So Dr. Stanley went back to the drawing board and looked elsewhere for the real millionaires. If they didn't live in the richest part of town, where could he find them? What he eventually learned was this:

1. **Real millionaires typically live in nice neighbourhoods in older houses.** They have learned that buying newer houses all the time is a waste of wealth. They like having a comfortable home in a regular neighbourhood, close to friends and family.
2. **Real millionaires drive nice cars, but buy them used.** They don't buy brand new, because they realize the best value is in buying a car that has lost its new car smell.
3. **Real millionaires are regular savers.** They don't become rich through good fortune. It takes time and hard work. They live below their means and use the surplus for savings and investment.
4. **Real millionaires are more likely to be business owners.** They're not generally found in what most of us consider wealthy professions such as doctors, dentists, lawyers, etc.

5. **Real millionaires don't spend excessively on vacations.** They spend their vacation dollars on reasonably priced family trips instead of high-end, exotic vacations.

Less than 10% of millionaires inherited their wealth. The vast majority started out like you and me and got there over time by applying good work habits and smart savings plans. Because they didn't live on credit, they were able to use their savings to start businesses that helped increase their wealth, rather than constantly moving from credit card to credit card.

As you can see, it makes sense to live a lifestyle you can afford. Here are three strategies for living below your means:

1. **Prepare.** Have an emergency fund with 2-3 months of salary set aside. Put aside money every month or delay the purchase of bigger items (e.g. vacation, new hot tub, home renos, etc.). You can also set up a Line of Credit with your bank that you hopefully never have to use. It's better to have a line of credit available than be stuck without one when you need it.
2. **Pay off debt.** Financially successful people don't carry a balance on their credit cards. Credit cards are for collecting points, not for buying things you can't pay cash for.
3. **Evaluate.** Every year, on December 31st, calculate your net worth to see how you're doing. There's a saying that what counts should be measured, and what's measured gets done. If you're measuring the size of your boat, you'll fall into a spending trap. If you're measuring your net worth once a year, you'll think about your finances differently.

Just like in the fable of the Golden Goose, being patient with your money instead of trying to get it all at once (i.e. live beyond your means) is the best way to ensure your financial success. The small decisions you make about spending your money today affect your long-term financial situation.

WHAT WE LEARNED:

1. Prepare for emergencies.
2. Plan ahead.
3. Evaluate your spending and net worth each year to look for bad spending habits that have creeped in.

Saving

Patty the Milkmaid was going to market carrying her milk in a Pail on her head. As she went along, she began calculating what she would do with the money she would get for the milk. "I'll buy some fowls from Farmer Brown," she said, "and they will lay eggs each morning, which I will sell to the parson's wife. With the money that I get from the sale of these eggs, I'll buy myself a new dress and a bonnet; and when I go to market, won't all the young men come up and speak to me! Polly Shaw will be jealous, but I don't care. I shall just look at her and toss my head like this."

As she spoke she tossed her head back, the Pail fell off, and all the milk was spilt. So she had to go home and tell her mother what had occurred. "Ah, my child," said the mother, "do not count your chickens before they are hatched."

CHAPTER AT A GLANCE: Saving is crucial to getting ahead — eventually you want your money to make money. There is no shortcut to it – you just have to start saving.

Saving is something you actually have to *do* – you can't dream about it or put it off until later. And the longer you delay, the smaller the eventual positive impact on your finances. So like the fable above, saving isn't something to dream about. One of the most common comments I hear from my clients is that they wished they had started their financial planning sooner. Whether it's saving, planning, retirement, or structuring an estate to minimize tax and probate costs, the earlier you start the better.

For example, if you want to save up to $1,000,000 by the time you turn 65, the amount you have to save per month changes dramatically depending on when you start, as you can see in the chart below.

How much you need to save to get $1M at retirement Daily or monthly investment suggested to build $1M by age 65			
Starting age	**Daily savings**	**Monthly savings**	**Yearly savings**
20	$12	$363	$4,354
25	$17	$502	$6,026
30	$23	$702	$8,423
35	$33	$996	$11,946
40	$48	$1,443	$17,316
45	$72	$2,164	$25,972
50	$115	$3,439	$41,263

We can always find reasons to delay saving (e.g. student loans, just married, first house, kids in sports, kids in university, etc.). My old boss used to tell his clients "the best time to start financial planning is when you're sixteen. The next best time is right now."

A successful saving strategy was popularized in the book *The Richest Man in Babylon* (a must read). Written in 1926, this fable is about a man who became the wealthiest man in Babylon. Two old friends called on him when they were having financial problems because they thought he could help.

His advice was simple, yet profound. Live on 90% of your income and put the other 10% into savings. While this seems hard to do, it is a guarantee of financial success.

Most people can't imagine living on only 90% of their income. But if you had to, you could. At some time in the past, you were living on less than you're living on right now.

Richard H. Thaler and Shlomo Benartzi of the University of Chicago published research in 2004 about the best way to help people save more. They found that people wanted to save more money in the future, but they didn't think they could get started today.

So the professors came up with an idea. They implemented a "Save More Tomorrow" plan where employees are invited to commit to gradually increase their savings over time. Every six months, employees increase their monthly savings by a certain amount until they reached their ideal savings goal. What the professors found was that when the sixth month came up, employees generally agreed to the increase in savings instead of cancelling it. They knew they'd made a good decision six months ago, so they let it stand. Or maybe it was that the effort to go to the employer to change it back was more than it was worth. Either way, it worked.

This type of savings plan could have a huge impact on your ability to save. So, talk to your employer or financial advisor to set it up.

WHAT WE LEARNED:

1. Make the decision to save — it doesn't magically happen.
2. Save 10% of your income to ensure financial success.
3. If you aren't saving 10%, think about strategies like the Save More Tomorrow program to get you to 10% savings.

Debt

An Ass was being driven along a road leading down the mountainside when he suddenly took it into his silly head to choose his own path. He could see his stall at the foot of the mountain, and the quickest way down seemed to be over the edge of the nearest cliff. Just as he was about to leap over, his master caught him by the tail and tried to pull him back, but the stubborn Ass would not yield and pulled with all his might.

"Fine," said his master, "go your way, you willful beast, and see where it leads you." With that he let go, and the foolish Ass tumbled head over heels down the mountainside and died.

CHAPTER AT A GLANCE: Debt robs you of future spending. So use it wisely or don't use it at all.

In the fable above, the Ass wanted to take a shortcut. Many of us do the same by buying things or experiences using debt instead of taking the time to save for it.

Just because there's a shortcut, doesn't mean you should take it. There's a great Saturday Night Live commercial parody called "Don't Spend Money You Don't Have." Steve Martin and Amy Poehler play a married couple who can't get out of debt. Chris

Parnell's character shows up to explain his program called *Don't Buy Stuff You Cannot Afford*.

Our grandparents saved up for things. Layaway plans helped people save up for things they wanted to buy. Now we do the opposite and feed our need for instant gratification — use credit to buy now and pay later. This easy credit and the pressure to keep up with the Joneses has caused many Canadians to mortgage their futures for the fleeting fun of today.

While credit cards can be useful, I see them abused *much more* than they're used. Here are some easy rules to follow:

1. **Never carry a balance.** If you can't afford to pay for something, then don't get it.
2. **Review your statements monthly.** Studies show that people spend 34% more when they pay by credit card than when they pay cash. Review your purchases regularly and catch poor spending habits early.
3. **Don't buy a big-ticket item the same day you see it.** Wait a week and if you still think you want it then buy it.
4. **Have one credit card.** Having multiple credit cards makes it easier to miss growing balances. You might also miss a payment and incur interest charges.
5. **Don't use a line of credit to pay off your credit cards**. This becomes a bad habit and while you might think you're using your line of credit wisely, you're just hiding that debt somewhere else.
6. **Understand that not all debt is bad.** The debt you use to buy your first home, start a business, or buy an investment can be useful. Instead of renting for 40 years and having nothing to show for it, the forced savings of a

mortgage and home repairs creates an asset out of an expense that you would have had anyways. That being said, I know some people who do rent and take their extra money and save it carefully which also results in a positive financial net worth. The problem is that most people who end up renting their entire lives don't do the extra savings.

7. **Borrowing to invest can be a good thing.** My Dad told me that every time he was less than $400,000 in debt to the bank, he felt compelled to borrow more and buy another asset. He knew that he could buy an investment (cows, quota, or land) that had a financial return greater than the cost of the interest. Most financially successful people I know have used debt to build up financial assets, usually through their businesses.

These financially successful people know that an asset is something that makes money. As Robert Kiyosaki of *Rich Dad Poor Dad* fame points out, most people buy liabilities. Things like cars and boats are rarely great assets. They may go up in value but there's an annual cost to owning them that usually offsets the gains. He says that your home is a liability once you add up all the costs of taxes, repairs, monthly expenses, etc. The cost of owning a house can be more than the cost of renting. I'm not sure I agree, but it's worth being aware of.

Instead, he recommends you buy real assets that appreciate in value. Businesses, real estate, or stocks all have the potential to appreciate faster than the cost of the interest on the debt.

A key part to debt management is knowing that interest rates are the thing that matters. There are some financial companies and advisors who would have you think that terms and payment are important — they're wrong. The amount of the payment, its timing, and its term are all secondary to the interest rate.

Another great tool for debt management is to change your monthly mortgage payments into biweekly payments. In effect, it's like making an extra monthly payment every year. The way to think about your mortgage payment is that the amount of interest you pay each year is fixed. So if you increase your payment in any way, 100% of that increase goes against your principle, reducing the time it takes to pay off your mortgage.

Also, prepaying your mortgage is always a good idea. If you can structure your prepayments around times when you don't have to pay a penalty, then great. But if you can't, it still doesn't hurt. The penalty is rarely more than the amount of interest you'd pay on the debt anyways.

I regularly get asked about saving versus paying down debt. Financially, you need to consider your tax situation (your tax bracket), the interest rate on the mortgage, what you're earning on your investments, and how long you have until retirement. So there's no one-size-fits-all answer. At times of low interest rates, a general rule is to be debt free by retirement, but it's not necessary to pay your debt off faster than that. If interest rates go above 5%, then I lean towards paying down debt.

WHAT WE LEARNED:

1. Be aware that not all debt is created equally.
2. Use debt to buy investments, not liabilities.
3. Pay attention to interest rates.

Taxes

A farmer's son was complaining one day about all the manure that he had to clean out of his father's barn. "Everyday it's the same thing – shovel, haul, dump. Shovel, haul, dump. Why can't my Dad do something about this?"

His Dad, overhearing the complaints, said, "Well son, we could get rid of all of our cows and then you wouldn't have to clean out any stalls at all. However, that would also mean we would have no milk to sell to our neighbours. And with no milk to sell we would have no money to buy food, pay our rent, or send you to school. So shovelling manure is your ticket to an education."

CHAPTER AT A GLANCE: Having a large tax bill is a good problem to have because it corresponds to a healthy income. But since it affects up to 50% of the income we make, it's wise to learn how our tax system works and what we can do to maximize the amount of income we keep.

I always start my tax seminars asking, "Who here would like to pay more taxes?" It's a rare person that will put up their hand to join mine. Then I throw the curveball — I tell them I'd love to pay more taxes because to pay more taxes, I'd need to make more money. High taxes and high income go hand in hand, like hauling manure and having money to get an education as in this chapter's fable.

When it comes to taxes, don't let the tail wag the dog; don't let a small issue control the big picture. Some people hate taxes so much they'd rather make less money than pay taxes. I've analyzed thousands of financial plans and there's one common theme: those who pay the highest taxes are the same people who make the most money.

There are many times I've heard, "I don't work overtime because it all goes to taxes," or "I don't want to work for the government anymore than I have to." While these statements *seem* to logical (and some maybe even think *noble*) they really show backward thinking.

In Canada, the most you pay on the money you earn is around 50%. So working overtime or getting a raise almost never results in paying more in taxes than you earn. Focus on making money first, *then* worry about taxes.

That said, paying less tax for a given level of income is a good idea.

In Canada, there are only a few ways to pay less tax. Since this book isn't meant to be a complete tax guide, I'll just highlight four concepts and five strategies for the average Canadian. Talk to your financial advisor or accountant for more personalized recommendations.

Here are some concepts around taxes you should know.

1. **Income based tax system**: Wealth taxes, such as the estate tax, are common in countries like the US, but not in Canada. Our only wealth tax is the probate fee you pay on death, but it's minimal (approximately 1.4% in BC), and there are some risks to trying to eliminate it.
2. **Marginal tax rate system**: A basic philosophy of Canadian society is that the more you make, the more taxes you pay. (Note: all numbers are approximate and vary by province). The first

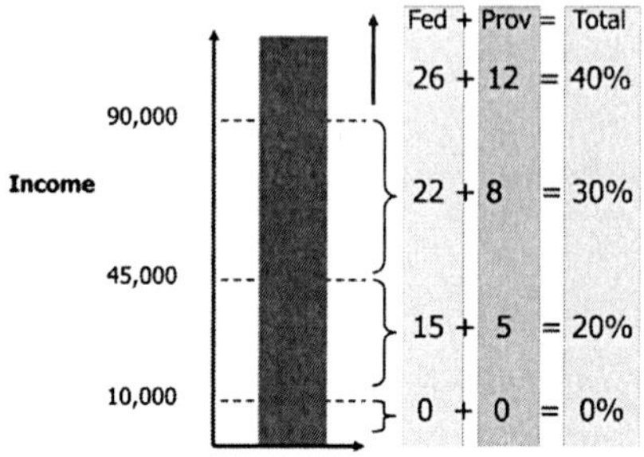

$10,000 you earn is not taxed, the next $35,000 is taxed at 20%, the next $45,000 is taxed at 30% and so on until it tops out at a marginal tax rate around 50%. The biggest misconception is that if you're in the top marginal tax bracket, your entire income is taxed at 50%. Wrong. No matter how high your income, the first $10,000 is still not taxed. This reality should help alleviate stress about moving up a tax bracket.
3. **Lower taxes for ownership investments**: The Canadian tax system is designed to tax the income earned on ownership investments at a lower rate. So GIC and bond income (loanership investments), which historically have the lowest returns, are taxed at the highest rate. Income you earn in the form of capital gains or dividends is taxed at approximately half the rate of interest income. This means that while capital gain and dividend

producing income may require more volatile investments, their favourable tax treatment can reduce risk considerably.

4. **Lifetime taxes**: Most income tax decisions are made only thinking about this year, not necessarily about the tax implications in the years to come. However, sometimes it makes more sense to pay some extra taxes this year to save on our overall tax bill in the future. Tax planning is best done while looking at the long term, not just today. For some people, deferring some income to a lower tax year through RRSPs (Registered Retirement Savings Accounts) will lower their overall taxes. On the flip side, it's a common tax mistake for low-income Canadians to use RRSPs — they're already in the lowest tax bracket so another saving's vehicles like the TFSA makes more sense. Other mistakes include overusing RRSP loans, failing to take advantage of income splitting, and not saving.

Based on these four main concepts, here are some basic **strategies** you can use to reduce your overall tax bill.

1. **RRSPs**: This is the most common tool for tax reduction used by Canadians. It defers the tax paid on income to a future year. For example, if you make an RRSP contribution when you're making $90,000, you'll reduce your taxes by $400 for every $1,000 you put into an RRSP. Then, when you retire and are earning $40,000 and are in the 30% tax bracket, you'll only pay $300 in taxes on every $1,000 you withdraw, which is a savings

of $100 (or 10%). So know your tax brackets now and in retirement to see how much RRSP contributions will benefit you.

2. **TFSA (Tax Free Savings Accounts)**: modeled on the Roth IRA from the US, this tax planning vehicle gives you no tax benefit when you contribute. However, the investment grows tax free and when you take it out there are no taxes to pay.
3. **Business ownership**: Economically, small businesses drive our economy, employ workers, and make wealth. Because of this, the government allows businesses a few more tax savings options, like income splitting, getting paid in dividends, and deducting expenses that are a result of trying to earn business income. The rules around businesses are more complicated, so talk to a professional before you start one up.
4. **Dividends and Capital Gains**: as mentioned earlier, investing your non-registered investments (non-RRSP and non-TFSA investments) to generate dividend and capital gains reduces your overall tax bite. Be aware that if you're collecting Guaranteed Income Supplement or Old Age Security, the tax treatment of dividends could negatively affect your taxes.
5. **Charitable giving**: One of my favourite money ideas is giving money away. My family does it regularly and we see the benefits for the charities contribute to. We live in an amazing society that gives us many benefits, and being able to share our good fortune with others is the best thing in the world. Not only is it beneficial for the receiver, it feels good for the giver, shooting our nervous

system full of positive chemicals like serotonin. The fact that you get a tax benefit is just another perk.

I've seen a myriad of other schemes designed to have people pay fewer taxes, from off-shore bank accounts to fancy charitable giving programs. In every case, the person gets caught and the government makes their life miserable with judgments and penalties. It's just not worth it.

So, the key to tax planning is to focus on making money through getting a good job, starting a business, and working hard (including overtime). And then make wise investments with your savings. Taxes are a by-product of making money, the same way manure is a by-product of farming. If you focus on making money first, your taxes will never be a problem.

WHAT WE LEARNED:

1. Understand the marginal tax system in Canada.
2. Plan your tax strategy long term, not just this year.

Inflation

There was a Farmer who was going to the Town Market to sell some goods so he loaded his camel with milk, eggs, and meat. Once the camel was fully laden, he decided that since straw was so light, the camel could take some bales of it too. Alas, despite the lightness of the straw, it was too much for the camel and it fell over with a broken back and died.

CHAPTER AT A GLANCE: The cost of living doubles every 20-30 years, so you need to prepare for it.

The cost of living changes over time, whether through food prices, gasoline, or housing. In this Arabic proverb, it doesn't seem like something nearly weightless like straw would break a camel's back. But I've seen the effects of inflation on the pension incomes of those who retired 30 years ago. It starts as a little increase in the cost of stamps and then suddenly, you can't afford to eat out anymore. So when planning for 20-40 years down the road, having an idea of the future costs you will encounter is very important.

There are two important concepts around inflation to understand. First, inflation is the cost of living going up over time. When I was younger, gas was 40 cents and a can of Pepsi was 25 cents. Now each costs over a dollar.

But there are some deflationary forces that reduce the cost of living. When I travelled Europe fifteen years ago, phone calls home were expensive. Now we have digital options like FaceTime and Skype. Computers and plasma TVs used to cost $2,000. Vacations to warmer climates were expensive and rare and today they're more accessible.

Despite deflationary forces, the overall cost of living has gone up by 2.5% per year over the last 70 years. There have been periods of time with high inflation (the late 1970s and early 1980s) and times when it's lower (the last 10 years). Governments use interest rates and the printing of money to affect the inflation rates with a common target of 2% annual inflation.

Financial plans have to include increasing expenses. At historic inflation rates, the cost of living will double every 20-30 years. So if you're 40, then by the time you are 65, you will spend twice as much money for the same amount of goods. If you live to 90, you'll spend four times as much money as you do today.

Thankfully, government pensions (like Old Age Security and the Canada Pension Plan) are currently indexed, meaning they increase with inflation. Many company pensions also include indexing and because of its impact on your retirement, you'll want to find out how your pension is structured.

There *are* some risks with pensions though. Bill Tufts and Lee Fairbanks in their book, *Pension Ponzi,* point out that many pension plans are failing to take into account lower rates of return and increased lifespans. Another factor impacting pension plans is that the ratio of contributors to beneficiaries is decreasing. And many public pension plans (pensions for government workers) are currently underfunded and it will be up to taxpayers to make up the shortfall. It's predicted that some municipal and state governments will get out from under this burden by declaring bankruptcy, divesting themselves of the need to make up any shortfall.

And if you have savings, you'll want to take inflation expectations into account when you start withdrawals. You may also want to save more or work longer in order to minimize the impact of inflation.

This may seem overwhelming, but we always adapt. If the cost of gas goes up too much, we will drive less. If the cost of meat goes up, we substitute with other foods. Already, many of my friends are eating less meat than previous generations. If travel gets too expensive, we'll vacation less or locally.

As people age, many find they spend less money. Their debts are paid off and they don't need to save anymore, which leaves more room for spending on fun things or just cutting back.

Inflation also impacts investments. You want your investments to grow faster than the cost of inflation or you won't be getting ahead. If our investments only grow at the rate of inflation, then we won't be getting ahead, which is why you need to get educated about investing options that can beat inflation.

WHAT WE LEARNED:

1. Be aware of how cost-of-living increases will impact your financial picture.
2. Check into whether your pension is indexed or not.

Insurance

A small boy was walking along a beach at low tide, where thousands of small starfish, having been washed up, were stranded and doomed to perish. A man watched as the boy picked up starfish one at a time and took them back to the water.

"I can see you're being very kind," said the watching man, "but there must be a million of them. You can't possibly make any difference."

The boy picked up a starfish and gently tossed it into the ocean. Returning from the water's edge, the boy said, "It will for that one."

CHAPTER AT A GLANCE: Know your responsibilities and ways to protect your loved ones in case something happens to you.

Like the starfish, insurance is a numbers game. For most of us, insurance will never make a difference. But for that one person who dies and leaves behind a family, or who gets critically sick and needs money to pay for extra medical care, insurance makes all the difference in the world. The thing is, we don't know if we'll be that one person.

Insurance involves answering the difficult question, *What would happen if…* What would happen if you got into a car accident and couldn't work? What would happen if you got cancer? What would happen if you died?

If you're a parent, you have children and maybe a spouse who are financially dependent on you. While the likelihood of you passing away is small, the impact would be huge. Life insurance allows people who share a small likelihood of an event happening (like death) to aggregate their money into a large pot where the unfortunate person who suffers a terrible event protects their family.

While some insurances (like car and home) are mandatory, I'm going to talk about the ones that are optional but have large financial impacts.

Life Insurance

This is the most common and most understood of the insurances. There are two reasons to get this kind of insurance. First, there are people who would be financially impacted if you were to pass away. In most cases, a simple Term Insurance policy is needed. This is a policy designed to be inexpensive, bought for a limited time (10-20 years), and when you're done, you can stop paying for it.

An example of term insurance is mortgage insurance, which the banks offer to protect themselves in the event a borrower passes away. The banks do not want to deal with the hassle of foreclosing or trying to collect their money from the surviving spouse. Unfortunately, there are three risks to mortgage insurance. First, because they don't verify your health until after you've died, the risk is that you've answered a question wrong and aren't covered. Second, the monthly cost of the insurance doesn't change, even though you are slowly (or quickly) paying off your mortgage. Third, because most mortgage terms are 5 years or less, if your health changes, then you won't be eligible for new insurance when you start a new term. Therefore, you should always get your own personal insurance through work or through a financial planner so you can lock in the costs and be assured of having the coverage.

The second reason to get life insurance is for its investment and tax benefits. Individuals who have a more sophisticated financial situation (family farm, business, holding company, or significant assets) need a more permanent insurance solution. Insurance policies have access to special tax treatment and can save estates thousands of dollars, especially in the event you're a business owner. In this case, a few pages are insufficient to explain how this works, so if this applies to you, make sure to see an accomplished Certified Financial Planner or Estate Planning Specialist.

Critical Illness Insurance

Many cancer, heart attack, and stroke patients suffer financially. This could be because of missed work (for both the patient and the family) or because some of the costs of medical care not being covered in Canada (like certain drugs or changing diets). These same patients sometimes choose to get faster medical treatment by going south of the border. In any case, the costs of having a serious illness can be mitigated by a Critical Illness policy which pays out a lump sum that can be used however you choose.

Disability Insurance

We all know people who've missed out on work because of an injury or illness; but thankfully, most of us are covered by either Workers' Compensation or a group benefit plan. This can be the most frustrating of the insurance policies because it's the most abused and easiest to cheat. Because it gets abused, you'll only be able to insure yourself for 70% to 80% of your pre-disability income.

Long Term Care Insurance

This insurance is associated with the costs of aging. When you become limited in your *Activities of Daily Living* (walking, bathing, toileting, mental cognition), this insurance will kick in and pay for some of the costs associated with getting additional assistance in your daily life. The benefit of being Canadian is that we will be taken care of to a minimum standard. But anything extra does cost money and unless you have a pension or significant assets, these expenses can really eat into the estate that's left for your children or charities. A private, long-term facility can cost approximately $5,000 a month, more than what most people's pensions will cover.

And many jurisdictions are doing income or asset based tests where the more money you have, the more care will cost. So far, the proceeds from Long Term Care Insurance are not considered income, so this saves your estate a lot of money.

Return of Premium

One of the best additions to Critical Illness and Disability policies is that you can add a Return of Premium Rider. This means that those who never claim on the policy will get all their money back.

The Final Word

Ideally, except for the Return of Premium Riders or Permanent Life Insurance Policies, insurance is something you get zero value from because the best-case scenario is that you never have to make a claim. But like the starfish fable, insurance will not benefit the majority of people. But for that one person who passes away (like the one starfish who is saved), insurance will make all the difference in the world.

And if you never make a claim, it means that the rest of your financial plan (saving and investing) is likely doing well because you've been healthy.

WHAT WE LEARNED:

1. Be aware of your financial responsibilities and what would happen if you died or couldn't work.
2. Buy only the insurance that you need.
3. Budget for insurance costs.
4. Get personal insurance instead of mortgage insurance.

Part Three:

Investing

Strategies for Smart Investing

Investing Basics

A Pigeon, plagued by excessive thirst, saw a goblet of water painted on a signboard. Not supposing it to be only a picture, she flew towards it and unwittingly slammed against the signboard, jarring herself terribly. Having broken her wings by the blow, she fell to the ground and was caught by a passing cat.

CHAPTER AT A GLANCE: There are many types of investments and none are perfect. Investments can be divided into two camps – lending money to earn interest or owing assets to earn profit. Over time, the latter is more lucrative.

The most critical part of investing is the ability to see through what seems obvious. Like the pigeon above, just because something looks a certain way, doesn't mean it's true.

Today, there are many inconsistencies in the investment world. Bonds and GICs were a reasonable investment from the 1970s to the mid 2010s. But interest rates were higher forty years ago and have been slowly falling. Today's low interest rates change return expectations.

"The Dow climbs a wall of worry," is an adage that explains a rise in the stock market during economic uncertainty, which seems to make no sense

With investing, you should always look beyond the simple answer. Be like the fox from a previous chapter. Learn lots of things, not just one.

There are many great investment books out there that go into way more detail than I want to go into here. So I'll give you a simple overview and a list of books you can read if you want to learn more.

The 3 Basic Rules of Investing

1. **We're hardwired to avoid risk.** The pain of losing is three times more intense then the joy of winning. This is why we really hate to see our investments go down in value — we fail to invest in good long-term investments because their short-term volatility makes us uncomfortable. The emotions around loss get in the way of making objective, logical long-term decisions.
2. **Every investment carries a risk.** Investing to eliminate emotional stress means settling for lower returns and a smaller nest egg in retirement. Investing to increase returns carries volatility risk. For some investors, risk is seeing their investment go down on a day or over a month which causes them to lose sleep. Others, such as Warren Buffett view risk as the chance that they won't get their money back. So Buffett is happy to buy a company (or stock) if he knows he's getting a deal and he ignores the volatility. If his investment goes down in

value the next day, he is ok with it because he knows that he bought an investment for a good price and eventually it will pay off.

3. **Know what you can control.** If you have a goal, you can either save more, spend less, or invest for a higher return. There is no magic. Investments that seem too good to be true, usually are.

All investments can be broken down into two categories:

1. **Loanership Investments**: These are loans made to banks, companies, or individuals. The interest rate you get is determined by the likelihood of getting your money back, government policies, inflation, and economic conditions. The safest investments have the lowest interest rates and these interest rates increase as the risk of not getting your money back increases. Usually the interest rate an investor earns increases as he/she moves from GICs (guaranteed investment certificates or term deposits), to government bonds, to mortgage funds, to corporate bonds, and to high-yield bonds.
2. **Ownership Investments**: These investments have the highest returns when measured over time. They include real estate, businesses, and stocks. Your returns come in the form of rent, business profits, and capital appreciation. Ownership investments are more complicated than loanership investments so you need to do more research. Historically (over longer periods of time), returns in ownership investments will be higher because you are taking on some risk in terms of volatility and uncertainty.

Because many people don't understand stocks, the third section of this book is dedicated to investment strategies. For now, here are some investing definitions:

Stocks, shares – Stocks are a type of security that signifies ownership in a corporation (business) and represent a claim on part of the corporation's assets and earnings.

Bonds – Bonds are a debt investment in which an investor loans money to an entity (corporate or government) that borrows the funds for a defined period of time at a fixed interest rate. Bonds are used by companies, municipalities, states, and governments to finance a variety of projects and activities.

Emerging Markets – An emerging market is underdeveloped relative to the advanced economies like Canada, US, Europe, and Japan. Emerging markets generally do not have the market efficiency and strict standards in accounting and securities regulation to be on par with advanced economies.

Commodities – Commodities (such as copper, steel, gold, oil, coal, etc.) are most often used as inputs in the production of other goods or services. The quality of a given commodity may differ slightly, but it is essentially uniform across producers. When they're traded on an exchange, commodities must also meet specified minimum standards, also known as a basis grade.

Mutual Funds – A mutual fund is an investment vehicle made up of a pool of funds collected from many investors for the purpose of investing in securities such as stocks, bonds, money market instruments, and similar assets. Mutual funds are operated by money managers who invest the fund's capital and attempt to produce capital gains and income for the fund's investors. A mutual fund's portfolio is structured and maintained to match the investment objectives stated in its prospectus.

Segregated Fund – Segregated funds are similar to mutual funds, except these are offered by an insurance company and have certain other advantages such as creditor protection and some death or maturity guarantees. Variable annuities or Guaranteed Minimum Withdrawal Benefit plans fall into this category.

Index Funds (or ETF) – A type of mutual fund with a portfolio constructed to match or track the components of a market index, such as the Standard & Poor's 500 Index (S&P 500) or the TSX. An index mutual fund provides broad market exposure, low operating expenses, and low portfolio turnover.

Mortgage Investment Company – A mortgage investment corporation or MIC is an investment company designed specifically for mortgage lending (primarily residential mortgage lending) in Canada. Owning shares in a mortgage investment corporation enables you to invest in a company which manages a diversified and secured pool of mortgages.

Investing can be learned, but for most people, their time would be better spent doing their own job. Learning the details that make a good investment portfolio takes time and effort — it's sometimes better to simply hire a professional to do it for you (like hiring a mechanic to fix your car).

In looking for a financial advisor, find one who's been in the business for at least one bear market and is younger than you (so that they don't retire before you do). Also, look for one who has a designation that signifies they've put in the effort to learn more about their job than the average advisor. Accredited advisors have demonstrated a commitment to their craft and they're doing more than just repeating the sales pitches their companies gave them.

Two common designations to look for are the Certified Financial Planner (CFP®) and Certified Financial Analyst.

WHAT WE LEARNED:

1. Take responsibility for your investment choices.
2. Learn the different investment options.
3. Choose investments that meet your goals.
4. Get help if you feel unsure about our own expertise.

Know the Risks

A Mule, laden with choice provisions of several sorts, was on his way to the field. His master and the reapers were at work there, and the provisions he carried were for the refreshment of both man and beast.

Seeing a large, strong thistle by the roadside, he stopped to eat. "Many people would wonder," thought he, "that with such dainty food upon my back, I shouldn't have appetite for the despised thistle; but to me the bitter, prickly weed has a more savory relish than anything else. Let others choose what they will, but give me a fine, juicy thistle like this, and I shall be content. Everyone to his own taste. What one rejects could be the choice of another. A wise man has said that a weed is a plant that people have not yet found a use for."

CHAPTER AT A GLANCE: Before investing, understand what you're doing. The biggest risk is rarely the investment, but rather how we respond emotionally to the investment's performance.

Risk means different things to different people. And investments carry different risks. Just like the thistle, which is good for the mule but bad for others, not everyone should invest the same.

Independent research company Dalbar has done many studies that show an investor's returns depend more on their emotional response to the investment than to the actual returns of the investment. This is because most people don't hold investments for the appropriate period of time. Investors usually buy and sell at the wrong times, which hurts overall return.

Historically, a common investment strategy has been to reduce exposure to stocks and increase exposure to GICs and bonds as you age. This strategy worked well for the last thirty years because of falling interest rates. But today, we're starting from a place of low interest rates. Investing in a 2% GIC means a million dollars generates less than $1,300 of monthly after-tax income. Given economic conditions today, this strategy doesn't look like it will work as well in the future.

We also have higher real estate prices. Thirty or forty years ago, on an absolute and relative basis, it took much less income to buy a house. This is not to say that house prices couldn't still increase, but the easy money seems to have been made.

Another investment strategy that's been questioned is Warren Buffett's buy and hold philosophy. It seems like ownership investments are more volatile than ever, so buying and holding a good investment isn't as simple. Also, with the faster pace of change, companies can go from stars to duds in a shorter time frame. The longevity of companies like Coca Cola and Disney are being called into question. They've been able to adapt very well over the last few decades, but will that continue?

The risk of ownership investments is also different based on your perspective. You may be like Warren Buffett and view risk as "the permanent loss of capital" — the day-to-day changes in the stock market don't matter to him. When Buffett invests in a business, he only worries about its ability to make a profit, not about the daily price of the stock. But some investors are more worried about the day-to-day volatility and lose sleep when there's the slightest fall in their investments.

There are many risks to investing, but not all investments have the same risks, and every investor views risk differently. There is not one particular investment that works for everyone.

It takes years of experience, mistakes, and successes to teach a person what works and what doesn't. It also takes years to learn the real risks of investing and whether you have the emotional fortitude to be a loaner or an owner investor. Don't settle for easy promises from investment advisors or websites. Learn enough about investing to know what you're looking for. Take time to know whose advice you can trust. And most importantly, try to leave emotions out of your investment decisions.

On January 5, 2015, Seth Godin wrote a blog post called *Uncertainty is not the same thing as risk* had this to say about risk, and it sums it up perfectly.

> *Often, the most important work we do doesn't bring a guaranteed, specific result. Usually, the result of any given action on our part is unknown.*
>
> *Uncertainty implies a range of possible outcomes.*
>
> *But a range of results, all uncertain, does not mean you are exposing yourself to risk. It merely means you're exposing yourself to an outcome you didn't have a chance to fall in love with in advance.*
>
> *A simple example: the typical high school student applying to a range of colleges has very little risk of not getting in anywhere. Apply to enough schools that match what you*

have to offer, and the odds are high indeed you'll get in somewhere. Low risk but a very high uncertainty about which college or colleges will say yes.

That's not risky. That's uncertain. It takes fortitude to live with a future that's not clearly imagined, but it's no reason not to apply.

Another example: If you speak to 100 people, it's uncertain which 40 people will be impacted by what you say. But the risk that you will resonate with no one is small indeed.

A portfolio of uncertain outcomes is very different from a large risk.

Many people view investing in anything other than GICs or term deposits as risky. Sometimes they use the word gambling to describe investing in the stock market. If you invest in a diversified portfolio of stocks, from a range of industries and countries, your actual return will be uncertain, but over time you'll get a positive, higher return than using bonds or GICs. It's the short-term, up and down path that your investments will take that's uncertain.

WHAT WE LEARNED:

1. Understand that every investment has some sort of risk attached to it.
2. Choose the investment risk that you want to take.
3. Do not confuse risk with uncertainty.

Understanding the Stock Market

A Crow, half-dead with thirst, came upon a Pitcher of water. When he put its beak into the mouth of the Pitcher, there was only very little water left and he could not reach it. He tried and he tried, but at last gave up in despair. Then a thought came to him. He took a pebble and dropped it into the Pitcher. Then he took another pebble and dropped it into the Pitcher. Then he took another pebble and dropped that into the Pitcher. He continued dropping in pebbles until at last he saw the water near the top and was able to quench his thirst and save his life.

CHAPTER AT A GLANCE: The stock market is where you buy and sell a portion of an existing business. Investing in the stock market is about understanding the underlying components of businesses and deciding which businesses are valuable and at what price.

We all know business owners who are wealthy. They took a risk, started a business, and now make a little bit of money on a lot of things. For the crow to raise the water level in the pitcher, the impact of one pebble was minimal, but when combined with a lot of other pebbles, the impact was huge. The same is true for businesses. Whether it's making a small bit of money on each shirt or iPhone app sold, each apartment rented, or each employee hired, a little bit on a lot of things adds up. The foundation of ownership investing is businesses. And the stock market is just a collection of businesses owned by a lot of people (the public).

Does it make sense to own businesses? There can be many things that go wrong in the short term, like a major customer going bankrupt, employee strike, mistake on an order, etc. But in the long run, businesses have proven to be profitable.

Businesses usually start out small, owned by one person, and serve the local community. But if Joe the plumber wanted to expand to serve the entire province, he might need investors to raise the money to buy more real estate, invest in more inventory, lease vehicles, and train employees. In this case, he needs to make his business more formal and find other investors.

So he divides the ownership of his business into equal pieces (shares) and sells some portion of them to other investors, who then share in the ownership, profits, and losses. As a larger business, Joe's Plumbing has the potential to make more profit to share among the new owners. So while Joe doesn't own the whole business and take 100% of the profit, he may own 25% of a business that is much larger, so his personal profit increases.

If a business gets so big that one individual and his friends can't afford to continue expanding, they need a way to meet other investors. This is the stock market, which is a collection of the world's largest companies with a wide range of owners, most of whom don't even know each other.

As these different owners buy and sell shares of the companies they own, they do it through the stock market. Based on their different opinions on the profitability of the businesses, the price of each business (share price) will go up and down. This results in the daily volatility of the stock market.

During the 1920s and 1930s, most people randomly picked stocks based on hype and news. To educate investors, Benjamin Graham, aptly named the Father of Investing, created a process to discover the real value of the companies he wanted to buy. He analyzed a company's balance sheet and income statement to come up with an appropriate value for each company. His research and analysis style was adopted by one of his students, Warren Buffett.

To teach his graduate students about the stock market, Ben Graham created the story of Mr. Market.

> *Imagine you are partners in a private business with a man named Mr. Market. Each day, he comes to your office or home and offers to buy your interest in the company or sell you his [the choice is yours]. The catch is, Mr. Market is an emotional wreck. At times, he suffers from excessive highs and at others, suicidal lows. When he is on one of his manic highs, his offering price for the business is high as well, because everything in his world at the time is cheery. His outlook for the company is wonderful, so he is only willing to sell you his stake in the company at a high price. At other times, his mood goes south and all he sees is a dismal future for the company. In fact, he is so concerned, he is willing to sell you his part of the company for far less than it is worth. All the while, the underlying value of the company may not have changed - just Mr. Market's mood.*

The best part of this entire arrangement; you are free to ignore him if you don't like his price. The next day, he'll show up at your door with a new one. For your interest, the more manic-depressive he is, the more opportunity you will have to take advantage of him (don't worry, he doesn't have feelings or mind being taken advantage of). As long as you have a strong conviction of what the company is really worth, you will be able to look at Mr. Market's offers and reject or accept them...the choice is yours.

This is exactly how the intelligent investor should look at the stock market – each security that is traded is merely a part of a business. Each morning, when you open up the newspaper or turn on CNBC, you can find Mr. Market's prices. It is your choice whether or not to act on them and buy or sell. If you find a company that he is offering for less than it is worth, take advantage of him and load up on it. Surely enough, as long as the company is fundamentally sound, one day he will come back under the sway of a manic high and offer to buy the same company from you for a much higher price.

By thinking of stock prices in this way – as mere quotes from an emotionally unstable business partner – you are free from the emotional attachment most investors feel toward rising and falling stock prices. Before long, when you are looking to buy stock, you will welcome falling prices. The only time you want to invite high stock prices is when you are eager to sell your securities for some reason. Thankfully, in most cases you are free to wait out Mr. Market's emotional roller coaster until he offers a price that you consider equal to or higher than intrinsic value. This is perhaps your greatest advantage in your investments.

The daily volatility of the stock market is Mr. Market at work. Whether he's happy or sad, his price will be high or low.

To measure the stock market in aggregate, averages or indices lump a certain group of companies into a big pot. Then we can more easily see the larger trends of many businesses and therefore the whole economy. The stock market moves up and down daily based on the mood of investors and the news of the companies. If there's good news today, the markets will typically move up. If there's bad news, then the market typically goes down.

Over months and years, an accumulation of good news tends to sway Mr. Market and the stock prices go higher and higher, until some catalyst causes the market to turn over and start to fall. Think 1929, 2000, and 2008 as points when investors had become too exuberant and subsequently, the stock markets fell. Conversely, in 1931, 1980, and 2009, pessimism was so entrenched that the stock market was trading at cheap levels, levels unwarranted by the reality. This is the challenge of investors – identifying if we're in a point of optimism, pessimism, or somewhere in the middle.

Looking at the TSX market data from July 1979 through March 2017, the market advanced on only 54% of trading days: a slight edge. This small edge on a daily basis, however, becomes a powerful advantage over longer periods of time. For example, the TSX advanced in 73% of the calendar years between 1924 and 2016. Further extending the time horizon, over rolling five-year periods, the TSX advanced 92% of the time, and over 10-year periods, 99% of the time.

Investing in ownership investments is about investing in businesses that sell products and services and participating in the profits and losses of those businesses. It's about finding good businesses and staying away from bad ones. It's about paying a fair price for the good businesses. The next few chapters will talk about strategies to make that happen.

WHAT WE LEARNED:

1. Look at the stock market as a group of successful and unsuccessful businesses.
2. Choose profitable businesses at reasonable prices.
3. Be aware of emotions — yours and others — that influence decision making.

Be Disciplined

Once upon a time there was a Hare who, boasting how he could run faster than anyone else, was forever teasing Tortoise for its slowness. Then one day, the irate Tortoise answered back: "Who do you think you are? There's no denying you're swift, but even you can be beaten!"

The Hare squealed with laughter. "Beaten in a race? By whom? Not you, surely! I bet there's nobody in the world that can win against me, I'm so speedy. Now, why don't you try?"

Annoyed by such bragging, the Tortoise accepted the challenge. A course was planned, and the next day at dawn they stood at the starting line. The Hare yawned sleepily as the meek Tortoise trudged slowly off. When the Hare saw how painfully slow his rival was, he decided, half asleep on his feet, to have a quick nap. "Take your time!" he said. "I'll have forty winks and catch up with you in a minute."

The Hare woke with a start from a fitful sleep and gazed round, looking for the Tortoise. But the creature was only a short distance away, having barely covered a third of the course. Breathing a sigh of relief, the Hare decided he might as well have breakfast too, and off he went to munch some cabbages he had noticed in a nearby field. But the heavy meal and the hot sun made his eyelids droop. With a careless glance at the Tortoise, now halfway along the course, he decided to have another snooze before flashing past the winning post. And smiling at the thought of the look on the Tortoise's face when he saw the Hare speed by, he fell fast asleep. The sun started to sink below the horizon and the Tortoise, who had been plodding towards the winning post since morning, was scarcely a yard from the finish.

At that very point, the Hare woke with a jolt. He could see the Tortoise a speck in the distance and away he dashed. He leapt and bounded at a great rate, his tongue lolling and gasping for breath. Just a little more and he'd be first at the finish. But the Hare's last leap was just too late, for the Tortoise had beaten him to the winning post. Poor Hare! Tired and in disgrace, he slumped down beside the Tortoise who was silently smiling at him.

CHAPTER AT A GLANCE: Discipline is the key to investment success.

The Tortoise and the Hare is a classic fable, but most people get the moral wrong. They assume that slow and steady is better than being fast. But think about it. Is there any way that a tortoise can beat a hare in a race if both are trying?

The hare lost because he was undisciplined. Being fast wasn't a bad thing. Rather, it was that falling asleep led to disaster.

The same is true with investing. There are many investments that will outperform GICs over time. But you have to have the discipline to learn how the investment works, understand the time frame necessary for success, and have the discipline to stick to a plan. There are no quick bucks to be made (or if it does happen, it's usually more luck than anything else). Don't fall for the idea that there are easy ways to make money.

One of the main reasons that investing in the stock market is extra hard, is because we're working against our own emotions. Inside our brain is a mini-brain called the amygdala. This part of our brain was developed long ago to protect us by constantly being on the lookout for danger and prompting us to fight, flee, or freeze. When you're being stalked in the jungles of Africa, reacting quickly to danger is a matter of life and death.

Today, that part of our brain doesn't have the ability to discern real from fake danger. The amygdala gets activated when we get our monthly statement and our investments have dropped in value. Or when we hear on the news that the stock market is down. Or when our investment portfolio has lost money.

None of these are life threatening, but our brains alert us every time it senses danger rather than be wrong one fatal time. According to neuroscience, not only is our amygdala on the lookout for physical harm, it's scanning for threats to things like our sense of control, status, and certainty of our future.

Real or not, when the fight-or-flight reaction is triggered, our bodies release adrenaline and cortisol into our bloodstream so we have the energy to get away or face our foe. For a gazelle being chased by a lion, this is really helpful. Once the gazelle safely out-runs the lion and the cortisol leaves her system, she relaxes and doesn't give it another thought.

Humans, however, continue to feel anxious or upset long after the event has passed, trying to figure out why it happened and how to keep it from happening again. Our bodies were not designed to handle this chronic stress. Since modern life is only going to feel more threatening, we need to learn how to reset:

1. **Get familiar with your personal fight-or-flight reaction.** Maybe your heart beats faster, your extremities get cold, or you feel nauseous.
2. **Realize threats as emotional triggers.** You feel a threat as a primitive, survival-driven reflex, not with your rational, thinking brain. You can choose what action to take instead of succumbing to your amygdala.
3. **Take a deep breath and tell yourself to "override" or "reset."** In fight-or-flight mode, we're narrowly focused on what's right in front of us. To shift out of it, we need to open our focus to a relaxed diffused form of attention so our brain waves calm down.

Dalbar, an independent investment research firm mentioned earlier, has studied investment returns and investor returns for 30 years. Whether investing in stocks, bonds, or mutual funds, they found that investors usually only experience about half the returns of the underlying investments. This was not because of fees or other costs, but because investors bought high and sold low (as opposed to buy low sell high). They followed the hype in the media and got into each trend too late.

The successful investor is not the one who picked the best investments. Instead, it was the one who stuck to their plan. As Warren Buffett says, "to invest successfully over a lifetime does not require a stratospheric IQ, unusual business insights or inside information. *What's needed is a sound intellectual framework for making decisions and the ability to keep emotions from corroding that framework.*" It's about learning how to override your amygdala, take a breath, and make a calm, logical decision.

I've seen this a few times in my investing career, where a very diversified and balanced investment portfolio is short circuited by the investor's emotions. One investor I worked for was not happy making 7% or 8% a year. Combined with the media fear around inflation and economic disaster, they moved their entire portfolios to gold and silver investments, which paid off handsomely for a while. But when gold and silver prices started falling in 2012, they were heavily penalized for being so concentrated in such a poorly performing asset class.

Other investors, when the market was at its low point in late 2008 and early 2009, decided to sell everything and exit the investment market. They couldn't handle the emotional stress of watching their investments fluctuate and sold at a low point. Looking back, each of those investors would have made up their losses and more if they had stayed invested.

The importance of being disciplined is about knowing what you can handle for investment risk. It's no good to invest in something if you don't have the emotional and intestinal fortitude to stay disciplined. One of my favourite sayings is that "there are no shortcuts to any place worth going." Investing is about a long-term, disciplined focus.

WHAT WE LEARNED:

1. Pay attention to your own emotions.
2. Have an investment plan and stick to it.

Diversification

An Old Man had many Sons, who were often quarreling. He tried to make them good friends, but could not. As the end of his life drew near, the old Man called them all to him and showed them a bundle of sticks tied tightly together.

"Now," said the Father, "see if you can break this bundle of sticks."

Each of the Sons took the bundle and tried with all his might to break it, but could not. When all had tried, the Father said, "Untie the bundle, and each of you take a stick and see if you can break that." This they could do very easily.

Then said the Father, "You saw when the sticks were bound together how strong they were; but as soon as they were untied, you broke them easily. Now, if you will stop quarreling and stand by each other, you will be like the bundle of sticks – no one can do you any harm; but if you do not keep together, you will be as weak as is one of the little sticks by itself, which anyone can break."

CHAPTER AT A GLANCE: Diversification is an easy way to reduce the risks of investing. It's about having a wide assortment of investments so that if any individual investment fails, you won't be sunk.

Probably the most commonly known piece of investment wisdom is the term diversification. We've all heard the advice to not put all our eggs in one basket. Like the old adage, "Two heads are better than one," the fable above is another great illustration on how the many are stronger than the few.

John Templeton said, "The only person who shouldn't diversify is one who is never wrong." And since I don't know many people who are always right, diversification is important. During the last four decades, we've experienced lots of economic uncertainty and I've read about many people who claim to have predicted this outcome or that event. Of course some of them were right, but none were right every time, picking the market tops bottoms. It's an impossible task, so don't believe anyone who tells you differently.

I remember in university, when the number 30 came up in my statistics class. The basic idea was that for a test or sample to have relevance, you needed to have 30 test subjects. If you polled at least 30 diverse people, their aggregate opinion on an election or idea would be something you could learn from. If you were measuring the accuracy of the machines in your factory, then you needed to sample at least 30 widgets.

In the investing world, it was no surprise to me to discover the same number. Researchers have found that investing in a minimum of 30 stocks is required to be adequately diversified. This drastically reduces the risk that any one individual stock going bankrupt will cause irreparable damage to your portfolio.

But the opposite can also be true. The ultimate un-diversifier is Warren Buffett. He believes that focusing on less is more. He states that having to know about hundreds of companies is an impossible task. I've recently been reading the Sherlock Holmes series by Arthur Conan Doyle. In one of his cases, Sherlock describes his brain as an attic with a finite amount of space. If you add a box to the attic, you have to take a box out. Buffett would agree that learning and paying attention to another company usually means that you're unable to follow a previous company. So, following too many companies is a bad thing.

There are two ways to approach diversification – the Buffett way or the index way.

The Buffett way is about careful research, investing only in companies selling for a reasonable price, and owning a reasonable number of these companies. The expectation isn't that you'll do better than the stock market this year, but that over time, you'll do as well or better, but with less risk.

The other option is to invest in an index fund. This is the ultimate diversifier. You don't pick any particular company — you pick them all. Studies show that this is effective because over time, markets do well. It takes up much less attic space.

I prefer Warren Buffett's way simply because I want less volatility. By investing in stocks that are already trading at a reasonable price, the downside is less. When the stock markets fall, which they do an average 25% of the years, a Buffett-like portfolio will fall less and your emotions won't kick in as hard. There is a cost to Warren Buffett's style of investing because the manager has to get paid. Index funds are cheap because it's simply a computer program doing the investing for you.

If you're a small investor, it's difficult to spread your investment into 30 individual purchases because the cost of making those purchases becomes prohibitive. So mutual funds were born where a group of investors pooled their money and bought as a group. Everyone shared in the profits and losses.

This has worked very well for the majority of investors who start out small. Until investment accounts grow to over $200,000, the ability to own your own shares is hard. And if you want to invest across multiple asset categories (i.e. Canadian stocks, Global stocks, bonds, MICs, etc.) then you need an even larger portfolio to still be adequately diversified.

Where I think investors get the short end of the stick is when they buy a mutual fund that's really just an index fund in disguise. You can recognize these funds because they're usually large and their mandate is to beat the index. Buffett-like funds rarely mention the index because they're trying to make money over time, not compete with something else.

So if you're using mutual funds, look for ones that have between 30 and 60 stocks and are reasonably sized. Funds larger than one billion dollars are usually unable to keep their holdings to under 50 because they'd be forced to invest in only the biggest companies or they'd have to diversify too much.

WHAT WE LEARNED:

1. Stay diversified.
2. Don't make big bets.
3. Use mutual funds or index funds if you are a smaller investor (under $2 million dollars).

Confirmation Bias

A little hungry Mouse found his way one day into a basket of corn. He had to squeeze himself a good deal to get through the narrow opening between the strips of the basket. But the corn was tempting and the Mouse was determined to get in. When at last he succeeded, he gorged himself to bursting. Indeed he became about three times as big around the middle as he was when he went in.

At last he felt satisfied and dragged himself to the opening to get out again. But the best he could do was to get his head out. So there he sat groaning and moaning, both from the discomfort inside him and his anxiety to escape from the basket.

Just then a Weasel came by. He understood the situation quickly.

"My friend," he said, "I know what you've been doing. You've been stuffing yourself. And this is what you get. You will have to stay there till you feel just like you did when you went in. Good night, and good enough for you.

And that was all the sympathy the poor Mouse got.

CHAPTER AT A GLANCE: We like to be right, so instead of working to learn, we put effort into finding others who already agree with us. This one-dimensional approach makes us blind to the big picture.

One of the biggest financial mistakes missing what's really there. Like the mouse who ignored the most important part of his situation (the size of the hole), many of us ignore the real picture because we only see what we want to see. Here are some examples:

1. **Our attention is drawn to the unusual.** Our brains are hardwired to fight, flee, or freeze. Wild claims by fringe ideas (blogs, rumors, cults, etc.) gain a credence they shouldn't have. This leads us to pay attention to the wrong things.
2. **Our brains seek out patterns, even when there aren't any.** This leads to the herd mentality that when the stock market is going up, it will go up forever. When it's going down, it will go down forever.
3. **Most people think that death by murder is common.** Instead, it's a rare form of death. But the news highlights murders all the time and skews our perceptions.
4. **We think the average person lives a pretty high standard of life.** TV sitcoms and dramas skew our thinking. Most people don't live in high rises with views of the Seattle Needle (Frasier) or live in 5,000 square-foot homes in Los Angeles (Modern Family). So we try to keep up with the Joneses who don't even exist.
5. **Those who get interviewed by the media usually take more extreme positions to catch our attention.** So those who are on the edges of politics (Tea Party and

Occupy Wall Street Protestors) get the majority of the attention when they are in fact the minority.

Studies show that those who make extreme predictions are less likely to be right than those who take a more moderate approach. But we rarely hear about the moderate approach. For example, in order to appear balanced, the media might look for two opposing views on a topic. If out of 100 analysts, 99 fall on one side of the issue, the media will pick one of them and pair them against the one who disagrees. When shown on TV as two opinions, we don't always see that the evidence is heavily weighted to one side. We think each side has equal credence when in fact, that may not be true.

Many of us have heard the adage, "Garbage In, Garbage Out." So what are you putting into your brain? If you watch the news every day, you're clouding your mind with negativity and the idea that the world is more dangerous than it really is. Studies show that the more news you watch, the less happy you are.

What does this mean for investors? Most of us are not day traders – so why do we care what the stock market did today? Watching BNN or CNBC just confuses us and causes us to make bad, emotional decisions. Part of the reason Warren Buffett lives in Omaha, Nebraska, is that it insulates him from the noise of Wall Street. He's always repeating the same mantra to ignore the stock market and focus on the businesses.

So don't get caught up in things that aren't true. Don't try to keep up with the Joneses — they don't exist. Don't pay attention to the stock market on a day-to-day basis. Don't believe the conspiracy stories.

We weigh facts and lines of reasoning far more strongly when they favour our own side, and we minimize the importance and validity of the opposition's arguments. This might be appropriate behavior in a formal debate or when we're trying to sway the opinion of a third party, but to the extent that we internalize these tendencies, they injure our ability to think and see clearly.

When it comes to investing, confirmation bias hurts us in two main ways. First, we'll believe something and only seek out or hear ideas that confirm it. For example, I commonly hear from investors that stocks are risky. But rather than engage in a discussion, these individuals rely on their emotions or past stories to limit their ability to see stocks from a different point of view.

Second, it hurts investors who've bought an investment and continue to own it, regardless of any new evidence or information that tells them that investment is now a bad one.

So don't get caught up in a set of economic beliefs or ideals. See what's really there. As Will Rogers said, "The fellow that can only see a week ahead is always the popular fellow, for he is looking with the crowd. But the one that can see years ahead, he has a telescope but he can't make anybody believe that he has it."

WHAT WE LEARNED:

1. Seek out differing opinions.
2. Do not assume you're always right.

Bucketing

A farmer's son was standing on the hilltop looking over their fields. He sadly turned to his Dad and said, 'What are we going to do? We have 18 fields to plow, then seed, then weed, then fertilize, then harvest, then store, then sell. How can we do all this?'

'Son, you are describing a whole year's worth of work. Let's parcel that out over all the days and just work on doing today what needs to get done. Separate the work into smaller chunks and you won't be so overwhelmed.'

CHAPTER AT A GLANCE: Separating our finances into smaller pieces makes it easier to manage. This is true for our spending (vacation account, new roof account, etc.) and true for our savings (short term savings account and longer term retirement account).

This is not a new concept and many people do it intuitively. They set aside a portion of their income for their various expenses – putting aside $200 a month to pay their property taxes every year, or $300 a month toward their annual vacation.

But it can also be used as a strategy with your retirement savings. Why? Because not all retirement dollars are created equal. Let's look at an example.

Let's say you are just retiring and you have $750,000. Some people assume those funds should immediately be moved to more conservative investments. Not so.

Assume that from these dollars, you need to generate $30,000 a year to pay for your retirement lifestyle. Let's look at a table.

Bucket	Year	Investment	Return	Amount
1	Year 1	Savings Account	0%	$30,000
2	Year 2	1 Year GIC	2%	$29,412
3	Year 3	2 Year GIC	2.2%	$28,722
4	Year 4	3 Year GIC	2.3%	$28,022
5	Year 5	4 Year GIC	2.5%	$27,179
6	Year 6-10	Conservative Balanced Fund	4%	$135,895
7	Remaining Years	Moderate Balanced Fund	6%	$470,770
			Total	$750,000

The next step is to review this annually and move portions of the money between the buckets as necessary. One year after the initial set up of this plan, the money in Bucket #2 goes into your savings account and becomes income for the next year. Bucket #3 has only one year left on its term and so becomes Bucket #2. The same is true for Buckets #4 and #5.

In years where Buckets #6 has done well, take $27,179 and move it from Bucket #6 and buy a new 4-year GIC and it becomes the money in Bucket #5. The same for Bucket #7.

If the investments in Buckets #6 or #7 haven't done well, then you can wait for a year when they do well. Looking back over the long history of investing (and even just over this last decade), the markets have not gone down for more than 5 years in a row. And they usually recover and exceed previous returns within 3 to 4 years.

This type of bucket planning is good for a variety of reasons. First, it creates certainty for your income for the next 5 and 10 years. Second, it provides the opportunity for higher returns over the life of your investment horizon. Most likely, your money will need to last 20 to 40 years and getting a good return is important.

To take this idea one step further, let's assume that you still only needed $30,000 a year, but you had $900,000 in savings. In this case, a plan would show that you only need $700,000 to maintain that income over the remaining years of your life. In this case, bucketing would dictate the extra $200,000 get invested with the time horizon of your children or your favourite charity in mind.

WHAT WE LEARNED:

1. Put your investments into different buckets with different investment goals.
2. Know if some of your money has a longer time horizon than your own life expectancy.

Socially Responsible Investing

A young Beaver was sent by his family to start his own home. He set out and found the prettiest little part of a stream he'd ever seen. There were a lot of trees around and he immediately started felling the trees and stripping the bark.

One day, his Uncle came along to visit. The scene of devastation was unnerving – every tree within a mile had been felled and lay ready to be hauled to the stream.

Coming up on his Nephew cutting down another tree, the Uncle asked, "What do you think you are doing?"

"Cutting down the trees to get them ready for my dam," said the young Beaver, "Why do you ask?"

"Cutting down all the trees will eventually destroy your home! With no trees, every rainfall will wash the soil away. You won't have any shade on the hot days. Where will your food grow the next year and the next? Your neighbours won't have homes nearby and you will be lonely. You might have a beautiful dam for a couple of seasons, but it won't last."

CHAPTER AT A GLANCE: Most of us make socially and environmentally responsible decisions when we buy things from the store and the same can be true when we invest. It's possible to make money *and* make a difference at the same time.

One of the more interesting aspects of human society is our ability to constantly grow. We've consistently pushed forward – whether it's in search of new lands, new science, or new technology. But we haven't been very good at tempering that insatiable appetite for more with the balance of social and environmental health.

Thousands of years ago, the Middle East was a vibrant, agricultural wonder, but through intense farming, that area has now turned to desert. London, in the Industrial Age, was so full of pollution that sewage and industrial chemicals floated down the Thames, poisoning millions of people.

And in the modern age, we've seen the effects humans have had on the ozone layer, smog in major cities, and drinking water around the world. Many of the problems we're fixing (ozone, smog, drinking water), but some are currently beyond our help (like desertification).

It's commonly accepted that we all do our part to reduce, reuse, and recycle. All these little things we do make a difference toward keeping our world a better place.

But did you know that you can also make a difference with your investments?

In addition to thinking about profits, we can invest to make a positive difference and minimizes the negative impact on our society. Socially Responsible Investors use the term "triple bottom line," to address the financial, social, and environmental impact of our investments. Not only are they trying to earn a respectable financial return on investments, they take the added step of asking 'what impact does this company have on our environment and on society?'

A second part of SRI (Socially Responsible Investing) looks at affecting positive change. I would say this part is the more important part today.

It's about proactively approaching companies, voting on issues, and presenting good ideas that go beyond just the company's goals around making money.

This can also be done through an investment practice of microlending. Commercial banks don't have the capacity or interest in making small loans to the world's poor. So creative programs have been developed to lend small amounts to those low-income populations where $100 can make a difference.

Many studies show the large positive impact an involved and engaged workforce has on a company. In Canada, we must look no further than WestJet where the employees are also owners. Their culture is filled with stories of employees going above and beyond to help a guest. Not only does this have a positive effect on WestJet employees in general, it generates extra profits through increased market share of the airline business in Canada. For more examples, look at Pike Place, Nordstrom, and Zappos.

A common misconception is that SRI investments make less money. Since 1990, the KLD Index (a proxy for SRI investing) has generated a return of 10.13% a year. The Standard & Poor's 500 index, the benchmark of the stock market, has lagged with an annualized return of 9.53%. There have been periods when the

KLD index lagged, such as 2005 to 2007, 2010, and 2012, but the overall trend is clear.

In Canada, the same study started in the mid-1990s with the Jantzi Social Index. Its results are very similar with a return very close to the underlying TSX index, with some years of outperformance and others of underperformance.

I wouldn't suggest that socially responsible investing will make you more money, but you can feel better about the money you make.

WHAT WE LEARNED:

1. Dig deeper into your investments and be aware beyond just their financial returns.
2. Choose investments that make money *and* make a difference.

Legacy

On a blistering hot summer day, a young man was sitting in the shade of an Oak tree taking a break from plowing his fields. He thought to himself, "If only my dad had done a better job at getting rich. Then I wouldn't have to work so hard seeding my crops in such heat."

The Oak tree, hearing the man's thoughts said, "Your great grandfather planted me a long time ago, because all he could think as he plowed the same field was, 'I hope that when my grandchildren grow up and plow this same field, that they will be able to take a rest in some shade during the hottest parts of the day instead of having to work in the heat as I do.'"

CHAPTER AT A GLANCE: All of us will have a legacy. What will yours be? Everyday, you're creating what you'll leave behind, so it's important to spend time thinking about it.

Your legacy will be what you leave behind. Hopefully it's something lasting, like an oak tree, offering benefits to following generations.

In financial planning, this is usually accomplished through saving money that you'll never use but will be passed onto the next generation. But it doesn't always have to be money. It can come in the form of education, values, or relationships that give children and grandchildren an advantage in their own lives.

In Canada, we're fortunate we don't live in a caste system or an uber-capitalistic society like the United States. Those types of countries have less mobility between socio-economic classes than we do. In Canada, we have access to a public education system that treats all students the same. But despite society's best efforts, reality is that children will still end up within shouting distance of their parents' socio-economic status. So the number one thing you can do to increase your children's socio-economic status is improve your own by applying sound financial principles to your own life.

As to specific ways you can maximize your legacy for your heirs, there are a few.

First, work at spending less than you earn and teach your children the same. Next, ensure that you'll never be a financial burden on your children. Plan for your own retirement, pay off debt, and invest wisely. Invest in your children's education through RESPs. Use your connections to help your children get a leg up in their business ventures, through financing or tapping existing relationships that help them get started.

Beyond your family, there's also the legacy you'll leave behind for charities. It takes the form of builders who start charities or those that build up funds and foundations that continue to fund a charity long after the original owner passes on. The most well-known legacy builder in history was Andrew Carnegie. In today's society, Bill and Melinda Gates, Warren Buffett, and Jim Pattison are also well known for their current efforts in attempting to leave our world in a better place than it is now.

Financially, here are the four key things you need to think about when it comes to your estate.

1. **Keep it simple.** The more complex your will or trusts you set up after your death are, the more accountants, lawyers, and financial planners will benefit. It will also take longer to settle your estate.
2. **Do the documents.** You need a will and a power of attorney and depending on your province of residence, a living will or representation agreement. These document your wishes when it comes to death, but also in the case that you become mentally incompetent from things like dementia, Alzheimer's, or a brain injury.
3. **Beware of taxes.** Thankfully, we don't have an inheritance or estate tax in Canada. However, on the date of your death, the government will assume that you sold all your investments which triggers a capital gains taxes. You will also have been deemed to close your RRSP or RRIF which is usually the highest taxed asset in estates. The exceptions to both of these is the opportunity to roll the assets over to a surviving spouse.
4. **Minimize your probate.** Probate in Canada runs around 1.5% of the value of an estate. Given the low cost, many solutions to minimize probate are risky. Putting assets in joint names with children can expose your assets to their creditors, unforeseen taxes, differences of opinion, or unequal inheritances. Instead, name appropriate beneficiaries, use insurance products, or gift money before you pass away. Be sure to get professional advice before trying to reduce probate on your own.

Finally, this is one of my favourite stories about the legacy that we leave our children. As we've all heard, values are caught not taught. Our children listen to what we say and how we live, so be aware of the messages you're sending. Parents have a strong hand in setting the financial and mental thermostats in their children's lives.

> *A retired Major League pitcher was visiting with some inmates at the local prison. "My Dad always used to tell me, 'Son, if you keep throwing the ball like that, you will play in the Majors someday. If you keep hitting like that, you will play in the Majors someday. If you keep running like that, you will play in the Majors someday.' And look at me – he was right."*
>
> *One of the inmates piped up and told the same story. "My Dad would always say, 'Son, if you keep talking back like that, you will end up in prison someday. If you keep lying to me like that, you will end up in prison someday. If you keep fighting with your brother like that, you will end up in prison someday.' And look at me – he was right."*

We all die (or at least the last time I checked we do 😊). The life we live will have an impact on those we leave behind, like planting an oak tree to shade our grandkids. Thinking about that impact and making more positive choices is important.

WHAT WE LEARNED:

1. Think about what you're teaching your family about money.
2. Have an estate plan, including a will.

The Value of Advice

Once there were two Frogs who were dear friends.

One lived in a deep pond in the woods where the trees hung over the water and where no one came to disturb him.

The other lived in a small pool. This was not a good place for a Frog or anyone else to live for the country road passed through the pool and all the horses and wagons passed that way, making the water muddy and foul. And It was not quiet like his friend's pond.

One day the Frog from the large pond said to the other, "Do come and live with me; I have plenty of food and water and nothing to disturb me; and it is so pleasant in my pond. In your little pond there is very little food, not much water, and the road passes through your pool. You must always be afraid of passers-by."

"Thank you," said the other Frog; "you are very kind, but I am quite content here. There is enough water. Those who pass never trouble me, and as for food, I had a good dinner the day before yesterday. I am used to this place and do not like change. But come and see me as often as you like."

The next time the Frog from the pond came to visit his friend, he could not find him.

"Too late." sang a Bird, who lived in a tree that overhung the pool.

"What do you mean?" said the Frog.

"Dead and gone!" said the Bird. "Run over by a wagon and killed two days ago, and a big Hawk came and carried him off."

"Alas! If he had only taken my advice, he might have been well and happy now," said the Frog, as he turned sadly towards home. "But he would have his way, and I have lost my friend."

CHAPTER AT A GLANCE: It's impossible to know everything and keep up in this information age. So get a trusted financial advisor to help you see the big picture.

There is value in advice. Like most twenty-year olds, I thought I knew it all. Now, every year, as I learn more, I look back and realize that I was never as smart as I thought I was. There's always someone who knows more, so I spend more of my time listening to others and asking their advice. This doesn't mean advice is always perfect, but the more you accumulate, the more discerning you'll become in deciding which advice to take.

A recent study of Canadian investors showed that those who used a financial advisor in some capacity had a $50,000 higher net worth than a person without an advisor. And US studies showed similar results.

This is because good advisors add much more than just investment advice. They look at an investor's total financial picture and find ways to save money in current spending plans and grow what's left. I've had clients whose banks are overcharging on their Lines of Credit without showing them how they could reduce it. I've seen investors saving into the wrong RRSP, not tax deducting interest on debt used for investment purposes, over paying medical expenses, or not using RESP's to save for their children's education. I've helped implement income splitting ideas that reduced a family's tax bill by thousands of dollars. I've helped business owners restructure their share ownership to reduce tax bills by 30%.

The recent birth of robo-advisors has raised some concern in the financial world. Good financial advice is more than finding the cheapest way to pick stocks, bonds, or mutual funds. There is value in knowing where to save money (RRSPs, TFSAs, RESPs), how best to pay off debt, how to minimize taxes, and how to maximize your estate. These are things that robo-advisors are not properly equipped to do.

Over the years, I've had the privilege of seeing hundreds of financial situations and read about thousands more. In the majority of cases, financial success comes from being slow and steady and making the right financial decisions on a daily basis. The get-rich-quick family is a rarity and the get-poor-quick one is much more common.

Either through ignorance, laziness, or bad luck, some families see their net worth fall by thousands and thousands of dollars through what I call the big mistake. The mistake is different things for different people. Some examples are:

- Investing in the hot stock your brother in law told you about
- Buying a house that's too expensive and being unable to keep up with costs
- Spending too much today and thinking you'll start saving sometime in the future
- Selling good quality investments because they're down and then not participating in the ride back up to prosperity

A good advisor is objective about your financial situation because they are not as emotionally involved as you are. I have my own advisors for my investments because I'm just like everyone else – too connected to my own money.

And, maybe most importantly, an advisor will correct the rumours you hear. I've heard tax rumours such as RRSP's don't work, not to work overtime, moving to a higher tax bracket is really bad, and that Canada has death taxes. I've also heard economic rumours about a one-world currency, exaggerations about US debt, and Chinese conspiracy theories. These rumours all have part truths, which make them so appealing. But believing them can result in making poor financial decisions.

Find a financial advisor you can trust and get on with the rest of your life.

WHAT WE LEARNED:

1. Find good help.
2. Focus on what you can control and what you're good at.
3. Get on with your life.

Planning Ahead

A singing bird was confined in a cage which hung outside a window. Unlike other song birds, this one had a way of singing at night when all other birds were asleep.

One night, a Bat came and clung to the bars of the cage and asked the Bird why she was silent by day and sang only at night. "I have a very good reason for doing so," said the Bird. "It was once when I was singing in the daytime that a fowler was attracted by my voice and set his nets for me and caught me. Since then I have never sung except by night."

But the Bat replied, "It is no use to do that now when you are a prisoner: if only you had done so before you were caught, you might still have been free."

CHAPTER AT A GLANCE: Planning for the unknown is hard — because it's unknown — but important. The consequences of financial mistakes can be huge.

My first boss had a phrase he used in all his financial courses. "The best time to plan for your retirement was when you were sixteen. The next best time to plan is now."

But like the songbird, sometimes you're caught in a challenging financial situation and it's too late. It could be an unexpected death in the family, a sudden change in your job due to downsizing, or a relationship that's evaporated. As Heraclitus of Ephesus said, "change is the only constant in life."

It's impossible to plan for everything that might happen, but some planning can go a long way to minimizing costs and disruptions from financial changes.

The first step goes back to my first chapter. Knowing where you are financially and where you want to go helps to lay out the steps you can take. Then doing some scenario planning (a business term) will show you some of the potential risks and holes in your plan.

Some of the most common financial disruptions are death, job loss, and divorce. I hope you're one of the lucky ones who escape unscathed, but most of us will get hit by or more of these.

One of the first things you can do is meet with a financial advisor, a trusted and experienced family member, or friend and ask for advice. If your spouse is up to it, they should be included, as it will likely be a problem for both of you.

Prenuptial agreements are becoming more common — even in first marriages — as we know half of marriages end in divorce. Pre-planning when both of you are calm and rational is much easier than waiting until there is acrimony and hurt.

Job loss is also a common disruption. Insurances like Worker's Compensation, Employment Insurance, or Disability Insurance go a long way to protecting you and your family. But what about job changes due to economic factors? You can work on building your network so you have people who can help if you lose your job. A friend may be able to help you find your next job.

Continually working on new skills helps — if the job environment changes, you can move to something else. A client who works for FedEx knows his job could become obsolete in the next 10 years, so he's starting night school to upgrade his computer skills.

Given how much society is changing and how expensive it is to get into the housing market, there's a chance that I'll need to work longer to support my family than I'd originally planned. I'm already planning to work beyond 65 just in case I need to. Do you have a job you could do beyond your normal retirement years if you had to?

A common mistake in estate planning is not thinking about how relationships will change when you or your spouse are out of the picture. I've seen estate plans that left everything to the two sons because the daughters had married well. How will that affect surviving children? What about a scenario where Mom is the glue that keeps the family together? When she's gone, will there still be family get-togethers?

What about when only one of the children has taken care of Mom and Dad? Should they be compensated differently from the estate? How do you communicate that to everyone?

What about second marriages when you want to take care of your spouse if you pass away first, but you also want to make sure your kids are taken care of?

And how do you want to teach your kids about the value of money. I recently got my son his first job. Thanks to the community I've built up over the years and the good will I've generated from being a hard worker myself, someone was willing to take a chance on my son. I don't want to wait until he is 16 or 22 for him to learn how to work hard.

One of my favourite bloggers and podcasters is Shane Parrish from Farnam Street (https://fs.blog). He's always trying to think about the bigger issues. To see the forest for the trees.

He wrote and article in April 2016 about "Second Order Thinking." It's actually quite difficult to do since we're inclined to see and only deal with what's right in front of us. We solve today's problem (child having a tantrum) only to realize later we've created a new problem (a child who regularly uses tantrums to get their way).

Shane quotes Ray Dalio, a successful hedge fund manager who says *"Failing to consider second- and third-order consequences is the cause of a lot of painfully bad decisions, and it is especially deadly when the first inferior option confirms your own biases. Never seize on the first available option, no matter how good it seems, before you've asked questions and explored."*

One of my favourite chapter titles of all time is "Don't let your kids do things that make you dislike them," from Jordan Peterson's *12 Principles for Life*. The basic idea is that if your kids are likeable, then people will help them. Others will look out for your children, giving them the benefit of the doubt, and offering them opportunities they may not have had otherwise. It's not about making them sycophants, but teaching them emotional regulation, respectfulness, and conscientiousness so others will want to have them around because they're helpful and kind.

But it's a difficult thing to do. When your children are having a tantrum in the grocery store, running around a restaurant, or breaking plates as they do the dishes, it's easiest to just ignore or solve the problem right in front of you. But what does that look like the next time and the next time?

When it comes to planning, don't stop at step one. Think about some of the potential repercussions down the road. "What if...?" is a great question to ask. When you're in the forest, it's hard to see the trees. So, as I mentioned in the previous chapter, get help. As a financial advisor, I've seen almost every type of financial situation. And your financial advisor has, too.

WHAT WE LEARNED:

1. Planning starts now, not later.
2. Think about second- and third-order consequences.
3. Ask for help — others will see things you're likely missing.

Focus on What You Can Control

A farmer had two donkeys, but not a pen to keep them in. So he hit upon a solution. He tied them together, assuming they wouldn't wander off. For a long time, he was right as when one tried to walk away, the other would stubbornly stay near the food. When the other tried to escape, the first stayed near the warm, dry barn.

A crow, seeing them struggle day after day, said, "why don't you work together. By fighting, the farmer ends up winning. If you want your freedom, you have to work as a team!"

CHAPTER AT A GLANCE: Know what you do and do not have control over. Most things are out of our control.

Fighting against forces pulling opposite of you is a struggle.

Maybe you have a partner who's a saver when you are a spender, risk averse when you are risky, or easygoing when you're focused. Like the donkeys, sometimes you can't win them over to your way of thinking.

I've worked with hundreds of couples and it's rare to have both partners on the same page. They discuss, debate, annoy, or fight, but eventually reach some sort of happy — or unhappy —

middle ground. Successful relationships usually have a few things in common. The partners recognize the difference, they give one person more control over some part of their financial picture (one spouse is in charge of investing or the budget), or they use a third party to help them navigate the decision-making process.

Another common example of working against immovable forces is fighting against things like taxes, interest rates, or US presidents. I haven't met anyone with a large influence on any of these issues. This reminds me of another fable.

> *The Wind and the Sun were disputing which was the stronger. Suddenly they saw a traveler coming down the road, and the Sun said: "I see a way to decide our dispute. Whichever of us can cause that traveler to take off his cloak shall be regarded as the stronger You begin." So the Sun retired behind a cloud, and the Wind began to blow as hard as it could upon the traveler. But the harder he blew, the more closely did the traveler wrap his cloak round him, till at last the Wind had to give up in despair. Then the Sun came out and shone in all his glory upon the traveler, who soon found it too hot to walk with his cloak on.*

The fable is commonly used to explain that kindness is better than force. But I also take it to mean that working *with* a situation usually has a better outcome than fighting against someone or something that won't relent.

In the case of taxes, the goal is to pay the least amount of taxes possible. But no matter what you do, you *will* pay taxes. So instead of spending energy (mental or emotional) on the unfairness of taxes, spend your energy on things you *can* control, like the amount of income you earn or making a tax plan. Financially successful people spend more time finding ways to earn more income instead of focusing on paying less taxes.

Interest rates and investment returns are another immovable force. As I mentioned in a previous chapter, investor behavior impacts over 90% of total returns. We're stuck in a low interest rate environment and while this might not be fair, an investor can't expect guaranteed, high returns. Also, volatility is a normal and expected part of investing in stocks, bonds, or real estate.

The same is true about our political leaders. I have two friends working on ulcers with an enraged focus on United States politics. They spend an hour a day reading and railing against something they have no control over (they can't vote in the US).

Government debt, jobs, trade wars, and real wars are just a few more things that we as individuals have little control over. I applaud anyone who takes the initiative to work on one or more of these issues. But if you're not in a place to make a change, work with the situation you find yourself in.

Don't be a donkey and fight against things you can't win.

WHAT WE LEARNED:

1. Work with the situation you find yourself in.
2. Not every issue in our lives is worth the fight.

The Final Word

At the beginning of this book I quoted the saying, "If ten coins are not enough to make a man rich, what if you add one coin? What if you add another? Finally, you will have to say that no one can be rich unless one coin can make him so." Life is about so much more than money. Money helps us live an amazing life and it contributes to so many things, but it's just a tool.

Being wise with your finances is not an easy process, but it's a simple one. Age-old adages around regular saving, balanced investing, and getting good advice are simple truisms. There are no proven shortcuts to financial success — it takes time and patience.

The journey of a thousand miles always starts with the first step, and the next and the next. In our culture of instant gratification, we chafe at the idea of slow and steady. But it's the only sure way to make it to the end.

Enjoy the journey.

Disclaimer

This book is written by Edwin Palsma in his individual capacity and not as a registered representation of Raymond James Ltd. (RJL) or any of its affiliates. It expresses the opinions of the authors and not necessarily those of Raymond James Ltd. This book is provided as a general source of information and should not be considered personal investment advice or financial planning advice. It should not be construed as an offer or solicitation for the sale or purchase of any product and should not be considered tax advice. We are not tax advisors and we recommend that clients seek independent advice from a professional advisor on tax-related matters. We recommend any individual seek independent advice from an investment advisor prior to making any investment decisions and from a professional accountant concerning tax-related matters. Statistics, factual data and other information are from sources RJL believes to be reliable but their accuracy cannot be guaranteed. This book is furnished on the basis and understanding that Raymond James Ltd. or any of its affiliates are to be under no liability whatsoever in respect therefore. This book may provide reference to third-party services. Raymond James Ltd. is not responsible for the availability of these external services, nor does Raymond James Ltd endorse, warrant or guarantee the products, services or information described or offered. Commissions, trailing commissions, management fees and expenses all may be associated with mutual funds. Please read the prospectus before investing. Mutual funds are not guaranteed, their values change frequently and past performance may not be repeated. Securities-related products and services are offered through Raymond James Ltd., Member-Canadian Investor Protection Fund. Insurance products and services products and services are offered through Raymond James Financial Planning Ltd., which is not a Member-Canadian Investor Protection Fund.